RIDING THE
WALL of DEATH

*From Ron & Viv
Father's Day.
June 2011*

Praise for *Riding the Wall of Death*

'A fascinating and unique insight into a part of entertainment folklore.'
World's Fair

'Full of narrative, anecdotes and historic images… a must for the fairground enthusiast and lovers of the Wall.'
Old Glory

'If you've ever enjoyed the Wall of Death then you'll love this book.'
Ken Fox, Ken Fox Troupe

'This book is well worth a read.'
Classic Bike

'A fascinating insight into what was once a hugely popular form of entertainment.'
Classic Motorcycle

'A worthwhile addition to the library of any fairground enthusiast.'
The Fairground Mercury

'This is a book aimed not just at bikers and fairground enthusiasts, its appeal goes much wider than that. Highly recommended.'
Amazon.co.uk

RIDING THE
WALL of DEATH

ALLAN FORD & NICK CORBLE

The History Press

Allan Ford would like to dedicate this book to the late Jim 'The Book' Parkinson

Front cover photograph commissioned by Tommy Messham Senior featuring Chris Lee performing the cross position while riding a 1927 750cc Indian Scout on Tommy Messham's Wall in 1976.

First published in 2006 by Tempus Publishing
Reprinted 2006 (twice)

Reprinted in 2009 by
The History Press
The Mill, Brimscombe Port,
Stroud, Gloucestershire, GL5 2QG
www.thehistorypress.co.uk

© Allan Ford & Nick Corble, 2006

The right of Allan Ford & Nick Corble to be identified as the Authors of this work has been asserted in accordance with the Copyrights, Designs and Patents Act 1988.

All rights reserved. No part of this book may be reprinted or reproduced or utilised in any form or by any electronic, mechanical or other means, now known or hereafter invented, including photocopying and recording, or in any information storage or retrieval system, without the permission in writing from the Publishers.

British Library Cataloguing in Publication Data.
A catalogue record for this book is available from the British Library.

ISBN 978 0 7524 3791 0

Typesetting and origination by
Tempus Publishing Limited
Printed in Great Britain

CONTENTS

	ABOUT THE AUTHORS	6
	INTRODUCTION	7
1	ROLL UP! ROLL UP!	9
2	LET THE SHOW BEGIN	23
3	THE GLORY DAYS	37
4	GOING ROUND	55
5	THE GLOBE	75
6	THE SHOW GOES ON	89
7	IN THE BLOOD	109
8	LAST CHANCE TO SEE… ?	125
9	PART OF THE CULTURE	143
	ENDNOTES	148
	WALL OF FAME	149
	SOURCES	157
	INDEX	159

ABOUT THE AUTHORS

Allan Ford is a name synonymous with the Wall of Death. He learnt to ride with Tommy Messham and went on to ride on Yvonne Stagg's Wall at the Kursaal in Southend and then Dreamland in Margate. When that Wall closed he rode in Iran before reviving the Wall in the UK, successfully running his Motordrome Company for over ten years, during which time it was the last travelling Wall visiting all the main outdoor venues. He still rides occasionally and is a keen champion of both the Wall and all things to do with fairgrounds.

Nick Corble is an established author based in Buckinghamshire whose first book *Walking on Water* was a canal travelogue tracing a trip down the spine of the inland waterways system. He has since written the biography *James Brindley – The First Canal Builder* and various canal towpath guides, all for Tempus. He also contributes regularly to the consumer press and has an interest in social history, walking, the waterways and biographies of ordinary people who've done extraordinary things.

INTRODUCTION

In an age when microchips, memory and megabytes increasingly rule our lives it seems a contradiction that something as raw and uncomplicated as the Wall of Death is currently undergoing a revival. The lesson seems clear: the appeal of the Wall is hardwired to quite basic instincts within us, instincts that transcend fashion and the fad of the moment and cannot be denied.

What are these instincts? At the core they include a human desire to challenge mortality, or more accurately to witness it being challenged, to be able to understand existence better by appreciating its boundaries. For the price of an entrance fee a visit to a Wall of Death allows those of us living more ordinary existences the opportunity to see life on the edge, with the ever-present possibility that life may be snatched away from someone at any moment. That this instinct is quite literally in our blood is confirmed as we watch a rider perform on the Wall and experience a rush of adrenaline, a primeval surge through the veins designed to protect us against danger.

Although this may be the effect, the reality is in fact quite different. Although Wall of Death riders do challenge death on a daily basis the odds are heavily stacked in their favour. The number of those who have died riding the Wall can be counted on the fingers of one hand – more people have met their end erecting or dismantling a Wall than riding one. This is to miss the point though. The Wall of Death is part of a much longer tradition, one of showmanship, of smoke and mirrors, of the triumph of illusion – of fairgrounds, colour, bright lights and release: a tradition of carnival and time spent in simple revelry that goes back centuries and meets another human need, that for pure unrefined entertainment for its own sake.

This is not to suggest that riding the Wall of Death involves trickery. In its early days Wall riders were accused of all sorts, of using magnets for example, to maintain their bikes on the vertical surface. These days knowledge of physics, of the centrifugal forces and properties of friction that in fact keep the bikes from falling, is more widespread, but this doesn't seem to dim our admiration. The combination of skill, flair and daring seems to override our rational side. We seem happy to suspend the sensible in favour of suspense – if only for fifteen minutes.

RIDING THE WALL OF DEATH

Nostalgia also has a part to play in explaining the appeal of the Wall. Even the bikes, the ancient skeletal Indians, come from another era and the riders themselves, often sporting fighter pilot-style nicknames such as 'Fearless', 'Speedy' or 'Cyclone', speak of another, perhaps more dangerous and exciting age, one we seem happy to pay to taste for a while.

As modern life becomes increasingly complicated the very simplicity of the Wall of Death provides a further attraction. What you see is what you get – men (and women) riding on the surface of a vertical circular wall: what could be simpler than that? Furthermore, at a time when entertainment has been specialised to appeal to only one or two of our senses the Wall of Death assaults all five: the smell of the oil, the sense of the Wall moving as the bikes go round, the acrid taste of the exhaust on our tongues, the sight, the unforgettable sight, of the riders circling below and perhaps most of all the sound, the echoing cacophony amplified within the large wooden drum that we carry ringing in our ears as we leave the show. There's nothing else quite like it.

These days the Wall has become a cultural icon, part of our heritage, a position it has cemented over nearly 100 years during which it has existed in one form or another. This book traces the early days of the Wall, how it started as a bicycle act and soon saw the potential of motorised bikes. How it invaded our shores and became a staple of outdoor entertainment between the wars, its riders the superstars of their time, and continued through the post-war period and weathered a period of decline before reviving in the early part of this century.

Along the way we look at the men, the machines, especially the mighty Indian, and variations of the act such as the Globe of Death. The story of the Wall encompasses showmen, murder, accidents and intrigue but most of all it reflects the history of entertainment through the last century and perhaps gives us an insight into ourselves.

We hope you enjoy reading this story and would like to thank all those who have helped us put it together, especially those whose contributions have allowed us to update this third edition. Many of these individuals are listed at the back of the book but special mention must go to Charles Winter for his knowledge and helpful comments on an early draft, Albert Evans and Ann Wright for access to their memories and archives and to Gerry de Roy, Neil Smart and others for putting up with our constant pestering for information and contacts. Where appropriate the source of photographs other than those belonging to the authors has been acknowledged. Any errors or omissions are entirely ours. They are, we hope, a small price to pay for recording the magic of the Wall.

Allan Ford   (www.thewallofdeath.com)
Nick Corble   (www.nickcorble.co.uk)

ONE

ROLL UP! ROLL UP!

Even from the outside it looks intimidating. A huge wooden circular drum topped off by a red and yellow segmented canvas point, wedged between a House of Horrors on one side and a Freak Show on the other. The visitor seems to have entered another world, one that challenges our understanding of normality, cloaks its secrets in mystery and hints at the fragility of life itself.

The wooden circle dominates this corner of the fairground. Steep stairs guard both sides, the bright-red gloss of their handrails glints in the sun and sends out a suggestion of dripping blood, while a raised stage at the front, its floor at eye-level to those outside, looks a bit like a mouth ready to swallow you up. Banks of multi-coloured light bulbs are dotted all around, flashing on and off and chasing around a sign that spells out the ominous announcement that the casual visitor has reached their ultimate destination: the Wall of Death.

No ordinary sideshow, the sheer scale and glitz of the Wall set it out it as the evening's brightest star and, should you have doubted it even for a minute, there's a tall announcer with straggling salt-and-pepper hair tied back in a ponytail standing on the stage commanding you to enter. 'This is the place to be,' he declares, his amplified voice performing a well-practised spiel giving you reasons to pause, listen and act, a litany he probably mumbles in his sleep, and may even, in time, be engraved on his headstone.

It's not always easy to hear what he's saying above the roar of the engines from the bikes that now line the stage. One of them is mounted on a set of rollers under each wheel of his bike, and the rider is gunning it for all it's worth. The odd word and phrase from the spieler, as he is known, cuts through the noise: 'unique', 'last chance to see', 'performing tricks you will scarcely believe', 'defying death'. It is the last word that resonates with the gathering crowd; death, the final and inevitable mystery, about to be denied.

RIDING THE WALL OF DEATH

Meanwhile, the rider on the bike up on the stage has let go of his handlebars and is standing up on his seat, while the two colleagues sharing the stage with him look on almost nonchalantly. They applaud each new trick almost mechanically as the rider goes through a repertoire almost worth the entrance fee in its own right. They've seen it all a thousand times before of course and can do each of the tricks themselves: putting their feet on the handlebars, sitting backwards, straddling the machine sideways, all the time keeping the bike upright and at a constant speed, but still they clap as if to give permission to the crowd that it's okay to do so.

'All the tricks you see before you now performed on the face of a wall as vertical as the walls in your home.' Incredible. Impossible. Worth a couple of quid of anyone's money to see, surely? The spieler gives an almost imperceptible nod to the rider to perform another of his tricks, judging to perfection the right moment to keep the gathering crowd's attention.

People of all types and ages have gathered in a semicircle in front of the spieler, with an advance party filtering off to the right to mount the stairs. A dad is propelled towards the cash booth by his two small children, one in each hand. They are innocent of death, but he is unsure if the show is appropriate for them. They are desperate to see the show and what dad could possibly refuse when, secretly, he is also keen to see if the show lives up to its promise? With practised ease the spieler provides the necessary reassurance: 'Suitable for all the family sir, children half price.' A woman inside the cash booth takes his money and he joins the growing sea of customers climbing the stairs.

A palpable buzz, sensed rather than heard, is now coming from inside the drum. A hatch in the side has been left open and from in front of the stage it's possible to see the bikes inside and a warm orange glow, as if the fires of hell have sunk into embers. The structure sways a little, not from the wind, which is negligible, but from the crowd inside as they jockey for the best view. What will it be like once the bikes get going? How safe are they going to be? Too late for those sorts of questions now.

To the sheer spectacle and the almost deafening sound can be added a blanket of petrol fumes, acrid and insistent, assaulting the nostrils, a fresh cloud thrown up each time the rider at the front opens up his throttle. The other two riders from the front have disappeared inside and are revving up their own machines, adding to the general cacophony and sense of chaos. It's clearly nearly time, and the spieler announces less than a minute to go in an effort to get the last waverers in, his voice maintaining its insistent monotone, repeating an earlier offer to refund the entrance fee to anyone not completely satisfied by the show, an offer no one has ever taken up in his thirty years doing this job.

Only he knows quite how imminent the show is but, as if to emphasise the urgency, the woman in the cash booth has a finger poised over the minute hand of the 'Next Show At' clock. The crowd out front has thinned, most of them now inside. The

ROLL UP! ROLL UP!

spieler's work is done and he turns his microphone off. The door is closed and the final section of the angled track that supports the base of the inner Wall is dropped into place. There's no escape now for the riders inside, and thick-set men in T-shirts guarding the exits suggest none for the crowd either. The sound of revving bikes becomes even louder, resonant, as if amplified by the wooden drum.

Inside it's as if everyone has entered some kind of dream-world, a feeling emphasised by the fiery glow that comes from above, the sun's rays filtered through the pastel shades of the canopy. The sound of gunshot peppers the air as one of the engines seems to continually misfire. Surely people really aren't going to risk their lives on those things? The machines look ancient, museum pieces, pared down to the absolute minimum and inexpertly painted a deep crimson red. Perhaps this is to stop the blood showing when they crash? The riders also look out of their time in their riding britches.

There are three of them in total, clustered around the hexagonal centre box from which protrudes the pole holding the canopy up. A slight ripple in the wind sends a wave across the roof, adding to the sense of something about to happen. For the dad with two children a macabre mix of anticipation, fascination and excitement combines in the pit of his stomach with a slight sense of the sort of guilt he might get if he'd slowed down to stare at a road accident.

Inside, all is wood. The Wall is constructed out of tall planks of pine with deep gouges across them, telling tales of times when things didn't go to plan. The smell of petrol fumes is now almost overwhelming. As well as the bikes there's a small go-kart built on a skeletal frame, little more than a child's toy. A driver's name is emblazoned across it like a signature, claiming it, a proclamation that only he is mad enough to drive it. Each of the riders is readily identifiable in their horse-riding breeches and matching T-shirts, the latter the same as worn by the bouncers at the exits. They don't look particularly special; you'd pass them in the street and not look twice at them, but they're ready to prove they can perform acts no ordinary man in the street would dare do.

The crowd gathers around the walkrounds that ring the top of the circle, looking down past a safety cable into the pit below. One of the riders steps up and picks up a fresh microphone from the table in the centre. He makes his introductions and confirms the spieler's promises that what the audience are about to see is something they will never forget before making his statutory safety announcements, a duty which seems almost superfluous in the circumstances.

A small forty-five-degree ramp track separates the floor from the base of the Wall and runs all the way round. Without further ado one of the riders kicks down his starter before removing it and handing it to one of his colleagues. Within seconds he's mounted the ramp and before he's even completed a circuit he's up on the Wall and the whole construction is oscillating from side to side each time he sweeps by, riding what seems to be a gravity-defying ninety degrees to the surface of the Wall. The crowd's heads swivel as one as they watch him circle the track below them.

Sections of the crowd keep pulling back as the rider seems to pick them out as a target, gunning his engine and sweeping straight up the side of the vertical Wall towards them, performing what the announcer calls the 'dips and dives of death'. Oscillating around the Wall, he opens the throttle and the machine beneath him misfires once more as he weaves up and down like a wave, his face blank but his eyes all-seeing. Already the crowd have got their money's worth; it looks as if that record of never having to give a refund is safe.

A huge part of the modern Wall of Death experience is the unique mixture it offers of ear-splitting sound, the pungent smell of petrol fumes and the physical swaying of the structure itself, all presented within a context of real and ever-present danger. It comes as something of a shock to discover, therefore, that the earliest incarnations of what we have come to know as the Wall of Death lacked the first three of these and didn't even feature motorbikes at all.

To get to the origins of the Wall, we have to go back over a century to the late 1890s and the heyday of the bicycle, which had revolutionised the public's perception of travel and speed. Cheap and readily available, bicycles captured the imagination of the common man and the 'middling-sort' alike, with hordes of enthusiasts taking advantage of increased leisure time to explore the countryside, enjoy fresh air and socialise.

As bicycles became embedded in the psyche fresh uses were found for these simple but effective machines. One suggestion is that the very earliest version of what was to become the Wall was as a circular track designed to allow the cyclist who wished to stay at home with a means to exercise, a sort of Victorian-era equivalent of a gym bike, and a precursor to the rollers used in modern Walls, although there is no documentary evidence to support this.

What we do know is that, by the time the century had turned, enterprising minds had realised the potential to use a similar device for the purposes of entertainment. One such invention, patented in 1901 by Charles Henry Jones, an ex-cycling champion of Australia and New Zealand, was known as 'Jones' Improved Course or Track for Cycling' and was described as 'a construction designed for use in cycle races or performances'[1].

The use of the word 'performances' here is interesting, as Jones' device was designed to be of specific use in 'music hall and other stages and places of public amusement and other places of limited area'[2]. The track Jones set out would be immediately recognisable to any modern-day Wall aficionado. Circular in shape, it consisted of a series of wooden slats raised vertically and supported round the edge with legs jutting out at a forty-five-degree angle for support.

ROLL UP! ROLL UP!

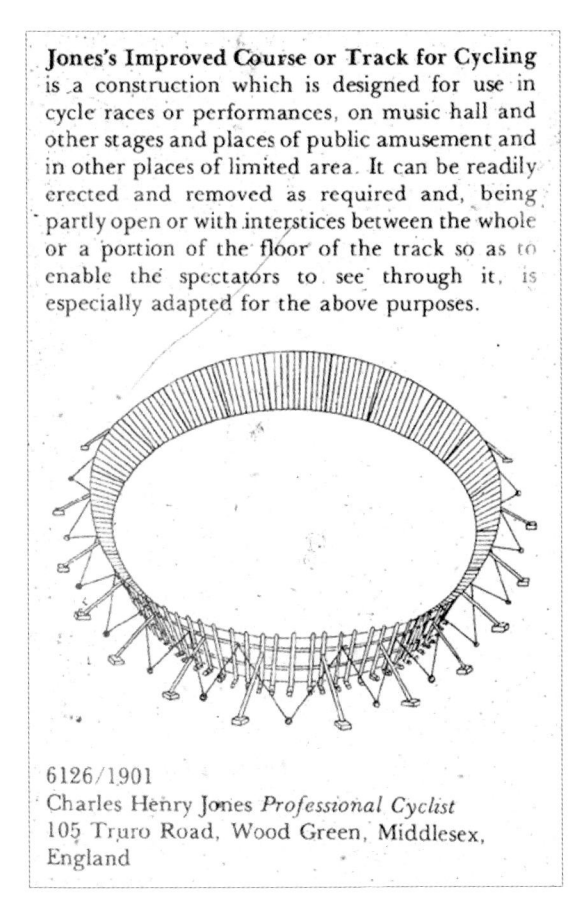

> **Jones's Improved Course or Track for Cycling** is a construction which is designed for use in cycle races or performances, on music hall and other stages and places of public amusement and in other places of limited area. It can be readily erected and removed as required and, being partly open or with interstices between the whole or a portion of the floor of the track so as to enable the spectators to see through it, is especially adapted for the above purposes.
>
> 6126/1901
> Charles Henry Jones *Professional Cyclist*
> 105 Truro Road, Wood Green, Middlesex, England

The patent for 'Jones's Improved Course of Track for Cycling' 1901.

What was more, the track was designed to be easy to erect and take down, and clearly wasn't intended to be permanent. The main difference was that Jones' slats were left partially open, to allow the audience to see through and enjoy the show. The track would be erected on a stage, with the paying public watching the action from their seats.

Charles Jones' track proved a big hit. In July 1902 Tertius Carr, a writer for *The Strand* magazine, reported on a visit to the show at the London Pavilion, to see what was now called the Jones-Hilliard Bicycle Sensation, and described what he called a 'gigantic soup-plate with the edges shaved off and part of the front sliced out like a Wedgwood card-basket'[3]. Eighteen foot in diameter, the 'soup-plate', as he called it, was raised up at an angle of sixty degrees, with each slat only five feet long. Contemporary photographs accompanying the article suggest that the slats were no more than two inches wide with the front half exposed to allow the audience to watch Jones' act, while the back half was covered with planks to allow him to pick up speed.

RIDING THE WALL OF DEATH

Carr described himself as 'conquered' by the act, a sensation familiar to subsequent generations the first time they witnessed the Wall of Death. Indeed, many of the elements that went on to make a typical Wall of Death act in the years that followed were pioneered by Jones and his team, giving him a fair claim to be the father of the show. The act was broken down into different sections, each one growing ever more daring and culminating in a challenge to the audience to ride the Wall, or soup bowl, a challenge that was never taken up.

Jones also employed a 'spieler', a front-of-house spokesman with the gift of the gab, whose job it was to talk up the danger involved and whet the audience's appetite for more. Wearing evening dress, this Edwardian showman, speaking as if he hardly believed it possible himself, described how Jones would ride 'at thirty miles an hour and without his handlebar, no power of guidance over his machine save his wonderful balance. See it before you believe it!' This was an act of audaciousness Jones was ready to commit every show.

Carr wrote how he and the rest of the audience stamped and clapped until they split their gloves. He was particularly impressed by Jones' finale, describing how he rode until he 'no longer looks like a man on a bicycle; he is a blurred line drawn round the track, and the track groans and protests… our hearts are in our mouths and we catch our breath as if we had swallowed a fly, for, in mid-career, he has made one wild jump from his machine, and is standing smiling and bowing in the middle of the card-basket.'

It seems the idea of paying to watch trick cyclists was a popular one, with a variation of the theme being the so-called 'Bowl of Death', significant for involving the first use of the idea of 'death' to inject a sense of danger and add a sense of showmanship. The bowls looked similar to Jones' contraption but were smaller in diameter, with the riders encouraged to ride up to the lip and perform their tricks from this vantage point so that the audience got a clearer view of them.

Again, many of these tricks would become familiar to later audiences watching Wall of Death shows, including riding standing up, side-saddle and with arms akimbo. Some even removed their clothes while spinning round the track, a trick Charlie Jones also offered to his audience. Another significant feature of the Bowl of Death was the fact that they were not confined to the theatre; being smaller they could be erected outdoors and they became popular at fairs.

The introduction of these new entertainments would have fitted the mood of the times. From being dens of iniquity, the music halls were the subject of a general clean-up during the closing years of the nineteenth century and had become considered safe for people of all classes to visit, although they remained particularly popular with the working classes. This was also an age of wonder, of new inventions and extravagance, when it had at last become acceptable to enjoy oneself in public, especially in Britain where the bon viveur Edward VII had finally ascended the throne after his mother's prolonged period of mourning for her late husband.

It was around this time that many of the outdoor entertainments we know as part of today's funfairs also began to take shape, with Edwardian inventors proving to be ever more ingenious in coming up with fresh attractions. Their appetite titillated by the sensation of speed afforded by their bicycles, the Edwardians relished the opportunity to partake of tracked rides, the forerunners of what became attractions such as the ghost train and water splash. These came to complement the ever-popular roundabouts that had emerged as the public's favourite towards the end of the nineteenth century, along with other steam-powered rides such as steam yachts, switchback rides and tunnel railways.

The more thrills the public were given though, the more they wanted. Ever-more entertainments were devised and cycles remained a popular focus for them. Another patent was lodged in 1904 by Tom Locock, a cycle and motor manufacturer, along with Tom Grave, and was described as 'a twister', which set out what can only be described as a giant hamster wheel or a Wall of Death on a spindle.

Called 'Lowcock and Grave's Trick Cycle Riding Apparatus'[4], the invention was intended to provide a platform for riders to display their skill and judgement, although little ever seemed to become of it. Another was the Loop the Loop, where the rider would describe a vertical circle by building up sufficient speed beforehand. Such cycling acts remained popular throughout the first decade of the new century, and continued to appear at funfairs and pier shows, but their days were numbered. As Tom Locock's occupation hints, the motorcycle was on its way.

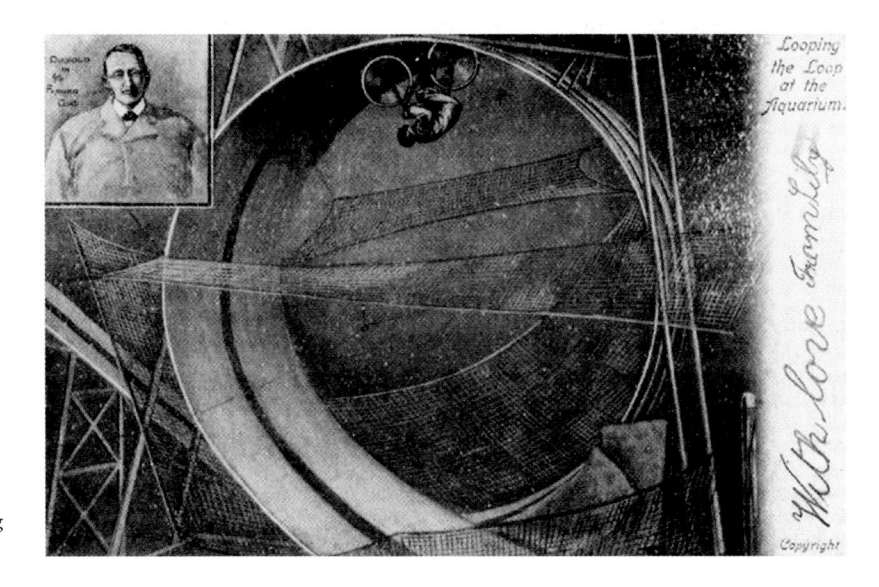

One of many variations of early cycle acts – Looping the Loop.

RIDING THE WALL OF DEATH

Trick cyclists pioneered many of the stunts later performed on the Wall.

The Lynton Troupe – a trio of cyclists trick riding on the West Pier, Brighton.

ROLL UP! ROLL UP!

The first motorcycles reliable enough for a showman to risk his neck on began to appear just after the turn of the century. As is often the way when it comes to entertainment, America led the way by adapting the wooden-board cycle tracks, stretching them to make them wider and squashing them into an oval, creating permanent racetracks not dissimilar from smaller versions of modern NASCAR tracks or speedway. These became big business, with receipts as high as $10,000 in a single day as early as 1910.

As bike engines improved and the machines got faster, so the temptation to build the banks up ever steeper followed, leading to increasingly dangerous tracks, which began to become known as 'Motordromes', although others chose to stress the sense of danger they were selling by adopting names such as 'Neck and Neck With Death'. Not only were the tracks becoming more dangerous, but the bikes themselves were stripped down until they became virtual death traps. With no brakes or clutch and carburettors run wide open to avoid the need for a throttle, the only way to control speed was an ignition cut out.

Accidents became inevitable, and perhaps the most notorious of these occurred at the Newark Motordrome, New Jersey, in September 1912 when six spectators were killed. A contemporary account of the accident described how the rider 'shot up the track at a sharp angle and struck the rail. He rode this railing for about a hundred feet and crushed out the lives of four boys who had been watching them with their heads far out over the rails.'[5] The bike went on to hit a fellow rider before smashing into a large post, whereupon the rear wheel detached itself and spun into the crowd, killing another spectator. The authorities were forced to act and it's perhaps unsurprising that the Newark track was closed, setting a precedent for others across the country in the following months and years, with board tracks replaced by the safer option of oval dirt tracks.

An early rider on these tracks was Erle Armstrong, an Illinois-born son of a mining engineer, whose family moved to Colorado in 1898 when he was ten. Six years later Armstrong was the Colorado State bicycling champion but, just as he achieved this status, his interest was drawn to motorbikes and he bought his first machine, an Orient. Two years later Armstrong began working as a mechanic for a Denver-based dealership with Indian Motorcycles, a name that in time was to become synonymous with the Wall.

Working every hour God sent, Armstrong earned enough to begin to race board-tracks, most notably the one based in Tuileries Park. Having won his first race and earned the nickname 'Red' for his brightly coloured hair, Armstrong went on to become one of the best riders in the Denver area and to become a factory rider for Indian. Before then, however, he had to survive an incident when a spurned lover speared a broomstick into his front wheel, causing him to crash, a warning he took to heart when he abandoned the perils of the single life the following year!

RIDING THE WALL OF DEATH

The Blanche and Diacoff trick cyclist act.

Early track racing at Milwaukee Motordrome, July 1913.

In 1915 Armstrong won a 300-mile endurance race in Tacoma, Washington in record-breaking time and decided shortly afterwards to get out while he was winning, in more ways than one, with the sport by that time having reached its peak in terms of danger. At this point Armstrong's story becomes typical of many of his contemporaries as he branched out into stunt riding, an occupation hardly less hazardous, but one more viable to a newly married man as the board-tracks began to be closed down.

Armstrong built himself a 'Silodrome', perhaps the clearest equivalent to the modern Wall and a name retained by the owners of many Walls in subsequent decades, one derived from the similarity of a Wall with a grain silo. Armstrong, however, had showman's blood in his veins and adopted the name 'The Whirl of Death' for his new attraction. Like the earlier Bowls of Death these were constructed out of wooden slats, although the greater speeds possible on motorbikes meant that they could be erected vertically. Again, like the Bowls of Death, sufficient gaps were left between the slats to allow spectators to view the show and the whole contraption was designed to allow easy build-up and dismantling. Once erected, Armstrong and another rider would perform going round the cylinder doing various stunts.

ROLL UP! ROLL UP!

In his first year with the Silodrome Armstrong was invited to perform at the prestigious Panama-Pacific Exhibition held in San Francisco using a much larger drome. As well as establishing the Silodrome as an attraction, Armstrong also began what was to become another Wall tradition by involving a woman, in this case his wife, in the show. At the Panama-Pacific the new Mrs Armstrong would ride on a specially built tandem motorbike, much to the delight of the crowd.

Armstrong's Silodrome was to be short-lived, however, as America's involvement in the First World War became inevitable, with Erle taking a full-time position with Indian running an Army motorcycle training school in Oklahoma, eventually going on to run his own Indian dealership and then becoming a production manager before his death, fittingly, in Springfield, home of the Indian, in 1978.

Before then, in 1914, the Parker Amusement Company, who owned several carnivals in the US and were better known for their carousels, built seven portable Walls, which they christened 'motordromes'. Fifty feet in diameter, these had spruce frames and yellow pine flooring although, like all early American dromes these were exposed to the elements, the 'tilt' or canopy a later addition. If it rained those running the drome would simply splash petrol on the water and burn off any excess moisture.

Realisation of the potential of motorcycles as popular entertainment was not confined to America. Some reports suggest that a rider called Charles Goddard rode a motorcycle in an attraction called the Wall of Death at a fairground near the Montparnasse in Paris as early as 1907. If true, this is both one of the earliest incarnations of the Wall as well as an early use of the name we now associate with the Wall, although it has also been suggested that some of the earlier motordromes also used this name and the leap from Armstrong's 'Whirl of Death' to 'Wall of Death' would have been shorter than Charlie Jones' finale leap from his cycle a few years before. Other, perhaps more partisan, accounts suggest that the term was dreamed up by British marketing men when the attraction finally found its way to these shores.

A possibly more fanciful explanation for the origins of the Wall of Death was put forward by Sam Naishtad, journalist and manager of the American Silodrome Riders Association in 1930, around the time the Wall was gaining popularity in Britain. According to this version of events an American saucer-track racer called Sam Anderson accidentally covered several laps of the perpendicular safety rail while cutting in on a rival. Anderson discovered the hard way that the only way was down but, undeterred after a spell in hospital, he tried to replicate his feat and in so doing 'invented' the idea of the Wall.

Although an attractive story, the Silodrome seems a more likely candidate, but the closest British audiences came to experiencing its thrills was probably acts such as the ones pioneered by the Tom Davis Trio and the Hall & Wilson Trio. Once again based in a theatre, Tom Davis' act began in 1912 when Davis, a successful champion

RIDING THE WALL OF DEATH

THE WORLD'S FAMOUS TOM DAVIES TRIO ON THEIR LEVIS'S

The Tom Davis Trio on their Levis, one of the world's first motorcycle stunt acts who went on to tour the world.

HALL & WILSON TRIO Thrilling Motor-Cycling Act, using LEVIS 2-STROKE MOTOR CYCLES.

Hall & Wilson Trio, another act using Levis, note the use of 'rollers' and the combination of bicycles and motorbikes.

ROLL UP! ROLL UP!

Staig's Original Motor Sensation – one of the early motorcycle stunt acts from Germany using Opel bikes. Note the poster for looping the aerial circle in English.

cyclist who had been performing in a bicycling act since the 1890s, was approached by a Mr Butterfield of the motorcycle firm Levis, who suggested that he may wish to spice up his show by using what he called 'motorised bicycles' made by his firm, no doubt to their mutual advantage.

The result was a spectacular show in which Tom, along with two colleagues, including his brother and, once again, a woman (and later a certain F. Bianchi), would ride round a saucer-shaped track very similar to earlier Bowls of Death, but with one crucial difference – it could be raised into the air, leaving the riders circling the track with nothing but a sheer drop beneath!

The bikes used by the trio were two-stroke factory machines with standard engines, the only adaptations being that they were fitted with pedalling gear and rigid forks. The tyres were 26 inches in diameter and 2 inches wide and the machines were fitted with a single brake. Tom Davis took pride in making sure that the bikes were presented in immaculate condition, their metal gleaming under the stage lights and showing them off to maximum effect. Critically, owing to fire regulations, they were also fitted with a removable rear tank filled with wadding. Just before a show this was filled up with petrol, soaking the wadding, and then any remaining petrol was tipped away. During the show the machines effectively ran off vapour through a flame trap.

RIDING THE WALL OF DEATH

Once again the Trio's show was broken down into sections, starting with a single rider riding round the 18-foot diameter track, the height a mere 5 feet with the sixty-degree angle employed. The slats were once again made of wood and had gaps between them. The whole contraption was broken down into four parts and could be erected in as little as ten minutes, a critical piece of timing as the act would have formed part of a wider show incorporating a number of different acts. Davis' act began with a single rider spinning round the track, typically Davis himself. He was soon joined by his female companion in the trio who proceeded to spin round the track in a form of race[6], again an element that later found its way into the standard Wall show.

Then things began to get interesting. The whole track would rise slowly into the air with the riders, still only operating on fumes, only kept from a potentially fatal fall by the laws of physics. The height of the rise is not documented but can be imagined as several feet given the height of most theatre stages. Then, as if this wasn't enough, the third of the trio would appear as if from nowhere, although in fact they used an unseen hole in the track, with the three spinning around in mid-air to the audience's delight.

Despite the undoubted ability of shows like this to capture the British public's imagination, few seemed willing to pick up the cudgels set down by the Tom Davis Trio. Davis went on to tour successfully for a number of years, but not in this country with audiences in America, notably at the Palace Theatre on Broadway, as well as in Australia, enjoying the thrills he offered in subsequent years. In a twist of fate, one of the Levis used by the trio, along with the track, was bought by Doug Murphy, a Wall of Death rider whose career is charted in later chapters, although neither was ever used again in a professional capacity and the other two machines remained in the ownership of the Levis Co. Much later, a section of the Davis track was given to Wall rider Allan Ford (author) as a memento.

Davis and his colleagues weren't alone it seems. A report in the 1913 edition of the Indian owner's periodical records the exploits of another trio, Will Wilson, Altona Edwards and George Botha, all South Africans. A picture of this Wall survives[7] and shows it lying at seventy-five degrees, with a diameter of 16 feet and a height of 15 feet. In the magazine Botha is quoted as saying that he 'will ride no machine other than Indian as my life depends upon its speed and strength', which, although it sounds like a plug, we can accept as genuine as it is a sentiment shared by subsequent generations of Wall riders.

TWO

LET THE SHOW BEGIN

In Britain at least, memories of the early motorcycle stunt riders risking their lives on vertical tracks became just that: memories, something that belonged to another, more innocent time. Reality had barged in and changed the context of the times, seemingly forever. The post-First World War era was different not only in terms of how people felt and thought about the world, but also on a practical level. Peace may have been everyone's dream but it came at a price, and a severe economic depression soon followed.

Suddenly, there was less money around for fripperies and entertainment. After a brief spell of prosperity, it proved difficult for Lloyd George's coalition government to deliver the promised 'land fit for heroes'. By the summer of 1921 over two million were unemployed, including many who'd survived the trenches, and inflation was rife. Survival was at the top of most families' minds. Matters continued to deteriorate after the collapse of the coalition and a run of short-term governments even more ill-equipped to cope with the deepening financial crisis followed.

Although some funfairs had kept going during the First World War, most had been cancelled and the economic situation in the immediate aftermath meant that few were brave enough to invest in fresh rides. Matters couldn't simply pick up where they'd left off; time was needed to establish a fresh equilibrium and repair the psychological and economic damage brought about by the conflict.

People continued to need diversions though and, despite no signs of improvement in the economic environment – if anything things got worse – the demand for amusement parks and fairs slowly recovered. It was almost as if a new normality had been accepted – things might be bad, but you've got to enjoy yourself sometime.

As the twenties progressed fresh and more inventive fairground rides were imported from America and, of all places, Germany – the two economies poised to overtake Britain in the industrial league in the next few years. Traditional rides such as scenic railways, steam yachts and gallopers gave way to the thrills of the 'Whip', 'Chair-o-Plane' and the 'Caterpillar', a fast roundabout that 'swallowed' its rider; with an increasing number of them powered by electricity rather than the traditional steam.

Even the Government got into the act. On St George's Day 1924 King George V travelled up from Windsor through fog and drizzle to the previously unheralded London suburb of Wembley to open the British Empire Exhibition. In true British tradition this had been the subject of controversy and delay and had proved difficult to finance, with most of its eventual £12 million cost having to be borrowed. The idea behind the exhibition was to revitalise the Empire and boost trade, but these weren't really notions that grabbed the common man's interest. What they flocked in their thousands to see was the amusement park.

All the new attractions were here. Visitors could experience the 'Flying Machine', an early form of aircraft simulator, the 'Hey Day', which gave the sensation of a serious motor skid, or the mile-long 'Grand National Giant Switchback', which was situated at the back of the hall and took two-and-a-half minutes to complete.

Notwithstanding these attractions, the official programme to the exhibition was clear that 'for those who enjoy watching thrills, the "Death Ring" provides the best.' This appears to be the first record since the end of the First World War of the reappearance of a form of the act pioneered by the Tom Davis Trio in the UK. The attraction was described as 'a cup-shaped steel cage [in which] a motor cyclist, and sometimes three, ride around the top of the track in a horizontal position and parallel to the ground.'[8]

The British public had rediscovered the thrill of watching riders defying gravity and performing stunts. The essence of the show at the British Empire Exhibition already bore the hallmarks of what was to become the Wall's standard act, starting with riders circling the lip of the ring and ending with three riders taking part in what we would now call 'the Hell Drivers race'.

The programme gives no indication of who the 'Death Ring' riders were and no subsequent record exists of what became of them and their act. It seems possible, however, that they were not home-grown, and possibly came from an outpost of the Empire or a country where the combination of social and economic circumstances was more favourable to developing innovative entertainment.

Fully fledged Walls began to appear in South Africa for example in the 1920s, and this country was to continue to have a strong Wall of Death pedigree over the following decades. One South African couple, Billie and Marjorie Ward, were known to have been touring a Wall in that country in the late 1920s, attracting the attention and admiration of no less an authority on speed and courage than the record-chaser Malcolm Campbell. In a letter from the Queen's Hotel, Cape Town, dated April 1929, Campbell wrote how he could 'safely say that your show is one of the most thrilling that I have ever seen', so much so that he went to see it several times. Interestingly,

LET THE SHOW BEGIN

Campbell also made note in his letter of the Wards' intention to take their show to Britain where, he suggests, 'to my knowledge there has been nothing like it'[9].

No such pause in development seemed to have taken place on the other side of the Atlantic. Silodromes were still doing good business in America, spawning a fresh generation of riders each trying to out-perform each other. One of these, twenty-four-year-old Louis 'Speedy' Babbs, hit upon the idea of setting an endurance record for the Wall, circling a drome at the Venice Amusement Pier on the West Coast non-stop for three hours and four minutes in October 1929, a feat made all the more remarkable by the fact that he refuelled as he went round.

Babbs will reappear later in this story and was a remarkable individual who enjoyed life on the edge – quite literally. He took up Wall riding after suffering a near-fatal accident in his first choice of career, that of aerial stuntman. His speciality was wing walking and, in 1927, he hit the ground hard after struggling to release a reserve parachute, necessitating a six-month spell in hospital. Despite this he alternated between the Wall and planes for the rest of his long career, on one occasion jumping from a plane strapped to sticks of dynamite and fireworks, which (perhaps inevitably) caused his parachute to catch fire.

No stranger to injury (he claimed to have broken fifty-six bones before retiring), three years after his record-breaking Wall ride he was to suffer another bizarre accident when demonstrating how to open a parachute safely for a Paramount News Reel. On this occasion a gust of wind from the propeller of a nearby plane opened the folds of his parachute and pulled him to the ground. Babbs was later to record that he got 'a concussion, a broken clavicle and a kiss' for his troubles.

Perhaps it was a result of this accident that, later on, Babbs focused more on bike work for a while and he has a good claim to be the forerunner to Evel Kneivel. One particular stunt he perfected was undressing down to a pair of tights while riding – and then getting dressed again, using the audience to hold his clothes, something made easier by the fact he refused to use a safety cable on his Wall.

Silodromes had continued to operate during and after the First World War in the US, with the dromes owned by the Parker Amusement Co. at the fore. Heroes from this time included the Purtle brothers, the most enduring of which was Earl Purtle, who was an early pioneer of trick riding following a successful spell as a dirt-track rider. At first American audiences had found the idea of motordromes a little bewildering, the idea of thrills and speed a little alien to the more innocent carnival atmosphere prevalent in that country. In the early days acts consisted mainly of two riders racing each other, but the Purtles soon worked out that if one of them could entertain the crowd with tricks the other could perform on the bally outside and drum up the 'tip' for the next show. The combination of noise from inside and a spieler on the outside proved to be a winning formula.

RIDING THE WALL OF DEATH

These were pioneering days. Earl experimented and taught himself some of the tricks that have now become a standard part of the Wall rider's repertoire, including riding side saddle. Experience also helped to form the shape of the drome itself, and Purtle was also one of the first to introduce the safety cable round the top of the Wall and the use of reinforcing cables to brace the outside of the walkrounds, necessary when the crowds began to build and the whole structure became unstable. He also introduced the tilt to keep off the rain. During this period of experimentation riders also adjusted the board round the inside of the Wall. Initially riders simply had a sloping starting-board, which left little room for chance, and this was soon replaced by a continuous sloping track.

By the 1920s Purtle owned two walls, one based at Palisades Park, New Jersey, and one on the road with the Cetlin-Wilson Carnival. The Park Wall was 33 feet in diameter and 14 feet 6 inches high. During this decade of experimentation Purtle also dabbled with both cars and lions, with the latter becoming a staple of his show for the next twenty years – always a lion called King and a lioness called Queenie.

Motorbike acts developed at separate speeds and in different directions in America and Europe during this time. In Europe riders and park operators seemed to prefer the open mesh cage or enclosure, most likely following a saucer shape, allowing the punters to gather around the attraction. In America evolution had gone down the route of the Silo or vertical solid Wall, with the paying public looking down on the riders from above. The Americans had also spent longer perfecting their show and showmanship and, possibly due to increasing competition within their own country towards the end of the decade, some ten years after the end of the First World War, some brave pioneers decided to pack their shows onto a liner and introduce them to the increasingly entertainment-hungry European audience. This was not a one-off occurrence; rather it was part of a wider trend that saw a range of fresh attractions come over the sea, with other examples including the perennial dodgems, first introduced by Billy Butlin when he was known more for his amusement parks than his holiday camps, and the Skid or Swirl, a version of the Whip.

It's not certain whose was the first American Wall to make it to Europe, and it probably doesn't matter too much as it seems likely that more than one proprietor had the same idea at the same time, with both the American Amusement Company and the Silodrome Company in the vanguard. The first of these advertised for recruits to its 'Wizards of the Wall' attraction around this time, a call answered by William 'Cyclone Billy' Bellhouse, a former speedway rider from Sheffield. Bellhouse went on to tour Europe from 1932-35, during which time he performed in Poland, Spain, Romania, Algeria and Holland.

Bellhouse later claimed to be the originator of many of the tricks that have become a standard part of the Wall of Death Show, including sitting on the

LET THE SHOW BEGIN

handlebars and steering the bike with his legs. Although undoubtedly a pioneer, given the number of riders around at this time it is unlikely that he was alone in performing these stunts, although he may have been the first to introduce them to European audiences. In a time of much slower communications, it is entirely likely that many riders were developing very similar stunts at around the same time.

Britain was ready for the Wall, and it wasn't backward in making up for lost time. The first written mentions of a Wall appeared in the trade journal *World's Fair*[10]. One of these referred to the 'Wall of Death, introduced to England this season' and featured a picture of two riders, Miss Pauline Crawford and Red Crawford, with the Wall in question, based at The Kursaal in Southend-on-Sea where a total of six riders rode. Two of these were the Wards from South Africa, whose act Malcolm Campbell had admired and the Wall itself was owned by Motor Silodromes Pty (Ltd).

Although this may be the first written mention of a Wall, the question of when it first appeared in Britain has been a periodic matter of debate in the letters pages of *World's Fair* over the years. From the earliest days correspondence has argued the case for a rival Wall at Belle Vue in Manchester being the first rather than Southend. This debate has continued and, although later correspondence in the 1970s is based upon recall and as such cannot be regarded as totally reliable, it is worth an airing.

One letter, from a George Purser of Ramsgate[11], claims that he joined a Wall at Pleasureland in his home town as a 'spieler-mechanic' in 1928. Equally, the post-Second-World War rider Albert Evans recalls his father, who also rode and was one of the first of the traditional fairground families north of the border to recognise the potential of the Wall, first seeing a Silodromes Wall at the Kelvin Hall in Glasgow in 1928. Although hard proof may not be available, it seems entirely possible that the Wall first appeared on these shores a year or two before its presence was formally recorded in the press. This possibility is supported by the evidence that it spread so rapidly from 1929 onwards.

The Ramsgate Wall, another owned by Silodromes Pty, was operated in that town and run by Auto-Rides Ltd on the old railway station site. The Wall stayed at Merrie England for the whole season before touring. The riders were 'Cyclone' Jack Cody, 'Captain' Bob and Marion Perry, the former an American, the latter a South African. Furthermore, one of the two owners, Joe Silverstone, was also a South African, the other being Bill Desnos, a Londoner.

Whether or not the first 'official' Wall in Britain came from America, there is plenty of evidence to suggest that this was the initial source of most of the riders and shows. That said, as we will see, British talent and ingenuity was remarkably quick off the mark to spot the potential of the Wall and take up the momentum. First, however, there was the little matter of solid wall or open mesh to sort out.

RIDING THE WALL OF DEATH

One of the earliest known photos of a Wall in the UK, taken at Belle Vue in Manchester, with the Wall known as the 'Drome of Death'.

The Perrys in action.

LET THE SHOW BEGIN

While waiting for the arrival of the Silodrome the evolution of the steel mesh saucer continued to its natural conclusion and became an enclosed sphere, known, predictably perhaps, as 'The Globe of Death'. The Globe became particularly popular in France, touring the continent before coming to Britain with the French Abbins brothers and becoming a well-known act. The history of the Globe is covered in more detail in Chapter 5, but it seems clear that, while it survived as a novelty act throughout the 1920s, it failed to become a mainstream attraction, partly perhaps, as we shall see later, because of the real dangers presented to those that rode it. What we do know is that when Walls of Death arrived on the scene they seemed to hit a different nerve. The experience of Albert Evans senior seems to be typical of showmen around this time. Despite still having his Globe, when he first saw the Wall he fell in love with it and knew he had to have one.

For a while Globes and Walls were often seen side by side and, even though those who saw them together usually agreed that although it was the Globe that offered the greatest thrill, it was the Wall that seemed to offer the greater spectacle. This was despite the fact that the new American Walls were shorter than the home-built variety that were to follow and were consequently more difficult to ride. From a showman's

Better known for their exploits in the Globe, Paulette and Henri Abbins were also French Wall pioneers.

perspective a Wall was also more efficient in terms of throughput, with a Globe usually requiring a tent around it to prevent others getting a free view, or forming part of a longer show possibly taking place in a theatre. In contrast, the audience for a Wall could be in and out in fifteen minutes, or even less if demand dictated. Furthermore, the Globe was inherently more dangerous and therefore attractive to a smaller pool of riders. Wall pioneer Billy Bellhouse's career was cut short through an accident on a Globe of Death, which was in fact his speciality, and he retired to run a fish and chip shop, a somewhat radical change of career. Although he later tried to claim compensation from his employer he was the victim not only of his accident but of the small print in his contract, which read: 'The director is not held responsible for any accident that may happen to his employees... during or resulting from their employment.'[12] His was not the only accident and, although the Globe was to avoid the fate of closure that befell board-track racing in America earlier in the century, indeed it has survived into modern times, it never really gained the same popularity as the Wall.

Whether it was reluctance on the part of the riders to tackle the Globe or the preference of showmen, or whether it was an example of the New World steamrolling European ideas, what we do know is that it was the vertical Silodrome Wall that grabbed the attention and stuck in the imagination. Almost overnight, fairs gained a new crowd pleaser, something completely different from the freak shows and rides that up until then had been the staple fare. It was a case of the right show at the right time although, as these pages will go on to show, the essential thrill of the Wall has proved remarkably enduring, not something specific to a particular time.

The Wall was an instant hit, not only with the crowds, but also with riders, proprietors and manufacturers. A whole generation of British Wall riders seemed to emerge as if from nowhere, many of them women, a tradition that has remained to this day. Indeed, the sheer speed with which this new cadre emerged lends some credence to the suggestion that the Wall, or something very much like it, had been around before it reached the attention of *World's Fair* in 1929. Learning to ride the Wall to sufficient proficiency to perform tricks is not something that can be achieved overnight – experts suggest at least a year is needed to achieve mastery.

Although the character and careers of many of the key riders from this era is covered in more detail in the following chapter, it's worth mentioning some of them in order to give a sense of the nature of this breed and the general atmosphere surrounding the Wall at this time. In particular, it is interesting to focus on some of the women who, along with Marjorie Ward and Pauline Crawford, were up there with the men leading the way.

Among other early 'Wizards of the Wall' were Lou 'Suicide' Cody, otherwise known as Curly (possibly related to Jack Cody), and a teenage rider called Winnie Souter, known

LET THE SHOW BEGIN

WINNIE SOUTTER.

Signed card from 'Fearless Wyn' Souter dated 1931. Wyn was one of the first of a wave of young women riders to take up the Wall.

as 'Fearless Winnie' or 'Fearless Wyn'. These two rode during the summer of 1930 at the Palace Gardens, New Brighton and their exploits achieved considerable press coverage at the time. The *Daily Mail* called their act 'the biggest thrill of all' and the *Daily Express* suggested the act was 'an astonishing exhibition of nerve and dare-devilry'. A poster advertising the show claimed audiences of 30,000 a week, although some allowance might be required for hyperbole as the same source announced that the riders travelled at between 60 and 100mph, where 40-50mph would have been more accurate.

That the show had grabbed the public's imagination seems irrefutable, as both royalty, including the Prince of Wales, politicians, including Ramsey MacDonald, and celebrity speed aces of the day such as Sir Henry Segrave and Kaye Don all visited the show. Winnie was a particular curiosity. Only fifteen at the time, she had begun to ride the year before when a pair of Canadian brothers, the Restalls, rented a flat over the corridor from her sister Gladys, who was working in the theatre at the time. The Restalls were ex-speedway riders, part of the North American wave of Wall riders, and were looking for women to join their show. The daughter of an insurance manager (although there was some music hall and acting blood in the family), Winnie already knew how to ride a motorbike as she lived with her grandmother and uncle at the time and the latter had been a speedway rider and had taught her. Reassured that the Restalls had a manager and were well intentioned, and by the fact that Gladys would also be involved, Winnie was allowed to take up the offer and her career was launched.

RIDING THE WALL OF DEATH

After her season in New Brighton Winnie joined her sister and another girl called Josie for a season in Scarborough, still riding under the 'Wizards of the Wall' name. In time, Winnie was to marry George Todd, one of four brothers who all became Wall riders, with each of them incidentally marrying Wall riders, as indeed did Gladys. As will become clear as this history unfolds, dynasties are a feature of the Wall, although this is more of a British phenomenon. The Restalls, for example, abandoned Wall riding to search for pirate treasure off Canada's Atlantic coast in the late 1950s, Robert Restall dying in the attempt along with his son.

Another early woman rider was Alma Skinner, known as 'Dare Devil Alma', from Rotherham. Despite never having ridden a motorbike before, she was captivated by her first sight of a Wall and, after pleading with Billy Butlin to be taken on, proved to be a quick learner. Previously a cashier on the distorting mirrors, where she earned 25 shillings a week, Alma was attracted to the Wall through a combination of the thrills and the money – she could earn £6 a week on the Wall. When Butlin asked if she thought she could do it she is said to have replied 'I'll have a bloody good try', at which point he tapped her with a stick and replied 'Go to it lass, you're just the sort we're looking for.'

Alma remembers this conversation[13] taking place in 1928, adding further credence to the case for walls being around before they were first mentioned in *World's Fair*. By the summer of 1929 she was riding at Skegness, her signature stunt riding being one leg draped over the handlebar, although she also rode blindfold, reading a newspaper and saluting, although not all at the same time. Simply being a woman, even the only woman rider, was not a big enough attraction on its own and Alma had to be at least as good as her male rivals with her tricks. Being female had its advantages though, and she cut a dashing figure in a white outfit set off with red boots, gloves and belt and red pom-poms.

While this generation of British riders was coming to the fore some of the original American pioneers continued to tour. Two of these, Fearless Egbert and Speedy Williams, a black rider, have some claims to be the first to introduce animals into the act, specifically a lion, which lay seemingly unconcerned on a board attached to a sidecar. In this case the lion simply patrolled the bottom of the Wall although, as we will go on to see, lions have earned a special part in the Wall's history and went on to achieve much greater heights – quite literally!

Another American rider was Bob Carew, who toured Europe from 1931, starting in Holland and ending in Russia where, with some prescience given the imminence of another war, he sold his Wall to some locals in 1938. Carew is credited with being one of the first to introduce the versatility of Indian Scouts to European audiences and, more importantly, to riders, and they have remained the bike of choice ever since.

LET THE SHOW BEGIN

Signed card from Fearless Egbert and fellow rider Jack O'Malley with their lion, riding on Collins' Wall.

An early British rider, Elias Harris, was a member of one of the fairground's leading families. Showmen, as they were known, tend to stick to their own and, through the Showmen's Guild, operated a virtual monopoly on pitches and rides for all the major fairs. It was no surprise therefore that Elias married the daughter of Pat Collins, the head of another, even more significant fairground family that had been the driving force behind the establishment of the Showmen's Guild in 1889.

Pat Collins had seen the potential of the Wall as soon as it was introduced and was quick off the mark to get one of his own. Collins presented both a Wall and a Globe at the Nottingham Goose Fair in 1929 and, subsequently, all of his shows featured both attractions, although they were actually owned by Silodromes Pta. It has become part of fairground folklore that Collins gave a Wall to Elias Harris as a wedding present, although there is no evidence to support this and it is just as likely that he acquired the Wall through a simple financial transaction when his wife died not long after their marriage. Harris rode the Wall himself with his son Anthony, who had his own specially adapted bike, thus simultaneously establishing one of the first Wall dynasties and a further Wall tradition of young riders. As an indication of his pedigree among fairground folk, Anthony later went on to become president of the Showmen's Guild.

RIDING THE WALL OF DEATH

One of the first Walls in Germany, where they were known as *Steilwands* – 'steep walls' – this one dating from 1930. Note the bally and spielers positioned above the crowd.

It was at this point that Billy Butlin re-enters the story. If Pat Collins was the face of the showman establishment then Billy Butlin was the new kid on the block. An amusement park entrepreneur (not only had he introduced dodgems, he had acquired the sole agency rights for them across the whole of Europe), Butlin had understood that people had become more mobile and were using the new charabancs for day trips, which they would save up for over a year. Whole factories or villages would travel as one, creating an alternative demand for amusement along the coasts, where most trips gravitated, and outside of the annual cycle of travelling fairs. The first of Butlin's parks was established with help from wealthy backers in 1927 in Skegness, just in time for the Wall.

Like Collins, Butlin was early to see the potential of the Wall of Death, although he retained the Silodrome name. The new attraction was perfect to pull punters into his new amusement parks, the number of which was growing rapidly with fresh sites appearing in Bognor, Clacton, Rhyl and Felixstowe. Butlin had also hit upon the idea of renting old factories and bus garages in the winter months to earn money

LET THE SHOW BEGIN

from his attractions all the year round. Unlike Collins, however, he needed to source his own Walls. It's at this point that another important name in the history of the Wall appears, that of amusement ride manufacturers Orton & Spooner.

Based in Burton upon Trent, Orton & Spooner was created from the amalgamation of two separate firms in 1925. The company's origins lay in woodcarving, specifically carving ship's figureheads, but they are best known for their later work in building showmen's caravans and fairground rides such as gallopers, switchbacks, ghost trains and roller coasters. Showing his by now customary flair, Butlin went to Orton & Spooner and secured a near monopoly of their output of Silodromes or Walls, a task that suited their woodworking skills perfectly. A near, but not total monopoly. Others also managed to secure some of the company's output during this time, including owners such as Eddie Monte, Albert Evans, Billy Grant and Albert Sedgwick, as well as Jake Messham and Pat Collins. In fact around this time there was a waiting list for Walls from Orton & Spooner and at one point Albert Evans allowed Billy Grant to have the next available Wall as he wasn't quite ready to present the act – a gesture he was to regret as by the time one was ready for him it cost a full £200 more!

Billy Lee and Ray James, a double act from the early 1930s dressed for the part.

RIDING THE WALL OF DEATH

Over time, Butlin is thought to have bought around twenty Walls from the company. Butlin's approach was to own the Walls but to rent them out to 'presenters' such as Marshalls or Greens, who would take the Wall, along with a couple of riders and maybe even a girl to ride round with, from Butlin for an agreed period or specific fair, usually for a percentage of the takings. At the same time, Butlin would keep some of the Walls on permanent sites in his growing empire of holiday camps.

Although walls originating from outside the country continued to tour, including those operated by the Silodrome Co. as well as the South African connection, the speed with which Orton & Spooner, along with local operators, got involved is testament to the grip the Wall of Death quickly exerted on the growing amusement industry. Although the national economic outlook remained bleak – the introduction of the American Silodrome to Europe coincided with the Wall Street Crash – fairgrounds and permanent amusement parks were about to enter their glory days.

THREE

THE GLORY DAYS

Suddenly there were Walls of Death everywhere – along with riders to ride them. Walls seemed to hit a collective nerve and the public couldn't get enough of them. It wasn't a case of 'seen one, seen them all'; punters would return to see a number of shows in the course of an afternoon, as if they couldn't believe what their eyes were telling them. Others may have believed what they saw, but came along to witness what was surely the inevitable crash. The logic seemed to go that the riders might have been lucky the first time they saw them, but the big smash might take place during the following show.

Where were these riders coming from? As the Depression gained a stranglehold on the economy, the prospect of becoming a Wall of Death rider was probably not all that preposterous. Not only did it pay well, but successful riders rapidly attracted fame and the attentions of young teenage 'groupies', two inducements that would have been more than enough to lure adventurous young men to the Wall. Others were speedway or dirt-track riders with proven bike-riding skills and a thirst for fresh thrills. Walls were the new thing, as professional riders they couldn't afford to ignore them. Yet more were stunt men or daredevils, drawn from the pool of daring young men as yet unburdened with commitments that exist in every generation. Some, including many of the most successful, seemed to appear from nowhere, attracted by the thrills and glamour and not always equipped with the knowledge of how to ride a bike. Like the boxing booths that often sat alongside Walls of Death, riding offered a rare and rapid opportunity for someone to pull themselves out of poverty and maybe even become 'someone'.

Not all of them made it however. Local riders were particularly attractive to the travelling shows – punters seemed more ready to pay to see a local lad risk his neck – and volunteers would often be recruited and taught the basics, although the best that could be hoped for in the short time available was to get them circling the track. For many this success went to their head; unwilling to put in the necessary hours they either drifted off, made mistakes or became too full of themselves and were kicked out.

Others were more successful – whether through hard graft or natural talent, or more often a combination of the two – and made a name for themselves. Billy Bellhouse and Cyclone Cody have already featured in this story, but there were plenty of others with them. Skid Skinner, husband to Alma Skinner, the novice who pleaded with Billy Butlin to learn how to ride, is another rider who made his name during the 1930s, presenting his own 'Bombshells' tour featuring three women, one of them his wife. A former speedway rider, Skinner became something of a star in his day, even modelling suits for Burtons the tailors at one stage.

Mention is also due to men such as Speedy Bob Lee, a 'Wizard of the Wall' who rode at Blackpool, and another 'Speedy', Speedy Bauer. The Todd brothers, Jack, Frank and George, were also early pioneers each with their own Walls, with a fourth brother Bob briefly lured into the act in the early 1930s.

Although using your status as a Wall of Death rider to attract young women may have been a strong inducement to some, it does not explain why so many women were themselves attracted to the Wall. What we do know is that this was the beginning of a new age for them. Votes on the same terms as men had been achieved in Britain in 1928 and the antics of the 'flappers' among the better off towards the end of the 1920s had perhaps shown those from more humble backgrounds that boundaries could be pushed, that women might have slightly more freedom than they'd previously supposed. The general profile of women had also risen; with so many of the men of their generation slaughtered, necessity had forced many young women into professions completely off-limits to their mothers' generation. Although probably not overtly conscious of a change in the social climate, enough young women appeared willing and able to grasp the opportunities opening up before them.

Both Winnie and Gladys Souter provide good examples of this phenomenon. Not out to prove a point or change the status of women, they were just independently minded young women attracted by the universal thrill of the Wall. In fact, most of the women who made their name riding the Wall in the 1930s were married to other Wall riders, including Alma Skinner and her husband Skid, and, as has already been noted, both the Souters went on to marry other Wall riders. Much like on the fairgrounds themselves, where there is and remains a strong tradition of inter-marriage between show families, the Wall was a closed world.

Winnie Souter's career is worth looking at in more detail as it provides a microcosm of the life of both a Wall rider and a woman rider during the 1930s. After spending the summer of 1929 at New Brighton, Winnie went with Curly Cody to

Wizards of the Wall, featuring Suicide Cody and Fearless Winnie Souter. (Courtesy Ann Wright)

RIDING THE WALL OF DEATH

Munich before joining up with her sister and a tank rider called Josie for a summer season at Scarborough in 1931, where she was known as 'Fearless Winnie'. The next two years were spent touring Scotland with Codonas before she joined the lion show at Barry in Glamorganshire. It was in Scotland that she met up with George Todd and they married in 1935, touring together over the following four years with Sam Naishtad acting as their manager until they bought their own Wall just before the Second World War.

If the new breed of riders was quick to materialise, the combination of traditional showman and eager new entrepreneur represented by Pat Collins and Billy Butlin respectively were equally quick off the mark. Butlin formed a company with Mark Loyd, brother of the MP Geoff Loyd, to operate and hire out Walls, while Collins' first Wall was unveiled to the public at Dudley in the Black Country. Following a successful court action against him by the Silodromes Company, Collins was, however, forced to drop the 'Wall of Death' name, but the hint at mortality and the dark side was retained by the new names he gave his attraction: 'The Death Riders' or 'The Drome of Satan'.

Orton & Spooner took orders for sixteen Walls, more than they could cope with, with much of the work being subcontracted out. A standard Orton & Spooner Wall cost £500, for which you got a 32-feet diameter drome, 18 feet high, made out of Canadian Red Wood. Each Wall was made out of eighteen sections and was secured together using bolts and wire ropes.

As we have seen, established fairground families such as Anderton and Rowlands, Codonas, Grants, Eddie Monte and Evans all managed to acquire their own Walls, often more than one, during this time, preventing a Collins/Butlin stranglehold on the act. Some ran as owner/operators, while others leased their Wall, typically from Pat Collins, while Butlins' Walls tended to be permanently stationed in one of his burgeoning empire of amusement parks and holiday camps. The introduction of Walls of Death also represented a shift in fairground thinking away from powered rides towards attractions, building upon an existing tradition of 'freak shows' and mini-music halls. Here the public paid to be entertained rather than to experience a thrill. What made Walls different was the combination they offered of the two: the public paid to witness an 'attraction', but one providing a thrill so powerful and immediate it was almost as if they were experiencing it themselves.

A typical lessee of this period was John Green & Sons, who were up and running as early as 1930. A typical deal around this time would involve the showman providing the labour, transport and sites, while the owners provided the riders and the Wall. Where the owners ran a number of Walls the riders would be provided from a pool, returning home in between shows. Unlike more modern riders they stayed well clear of the job of moving, erecting and selling the show, a way of working that only added to their exulted status.

THE GLORY DAYS

In between shows the star riders would get to stay in local railway hotels, but those lower down the scale would either eat and sleep in the fair or lodge at a local cottage. The experience of Wall rider Bill Tayleur, aka 'Garlicky Bill the Tayleur', would have been typical of the lot of most around this time[14]. He describes how he could never eat a square meal during the day because 'it felt like a cannon ball in one's stomach' when he rode. His main meal would come late at night, usually after midnight and, if staying on the tober (site), this would probably consist of 'plates of squashy peas and saucers of whelks that tasted like India rubber'. Those staying in the hotels would get fed mutton followed by rice pudding, but the best Bill could hope for was a berth in a miner's cottage, where the miner's wife would leave 'summat hot in t'oven', often tripe and cow heel stewed in milk with onions.

Lessees might therefore get different riders each week, and an early tradition was formed of showmen themselves or their sons riding the Wall to cut costs and improve reliability – jobbing riders weren't the most reliable of people. Takings were split 50/50, with operators obliged to keep strict records of the number of punters through the gate. This may go some way to explaining the origins of the practice of soliciting 'nobbins', a feature of a Wall show that has never gone away and is now firmly enshrined in Wall of Death tradition. Having witnessed the show one of the riders would address the audience directly. The spiel varied very little from show to show and typically went something like: 'Given the daring nature of what we do, no insurance company in the world will insure us, so we have started a small fund for those injured for your entertainment and to support our widows and children.' Having softened up the customer's conscience, the spiel would go on, 'If you have enjoyed our death-defying performance perhaps you would like to support our fund by throwing your contributions into the Wall.'

A shower of coins would typically follow, dodged good-naturedly and with gratitude by those waiting in the pit below. The nobbins were swept and collected at the end of the evening, with coins lodged in between boards traditionally left for the chaps or roustabouts whose job it was to dismantle the Wall.

This arrangement did not guarantee profits, and Greens only ran a Wall for a year, during which riders such as Speedy Towers, Cyclone Anderson, Dare Devil Joyce and Bobby Hayhurst all plied their trade. Around this time the tradition of adopting some kind of sobriquet became firmly established, with many taking their inspiration from the new breed of air aces also coming to the fore. Even if Green & Sons had decided they wanted to try other things, plenty of others were ready and waiting to take their place, with an enterprising soul called Joe Markland helping them on their way after measuring Greens' Wall while it was on the trucks at the Wigan October Fair and going on to make Walls for Grants and Albert Evans, although to

Riders posing with a car as early as 1931 at Stratford. The sign on the left describes 'Human Flies Cheating the Undertaker'.

a slightly modified design. Then as now, there was no 'standard' dimension for a Wall. Bill Tayleur described his Wall as only 30 feet in diameter, but 30 feet high, built out of twenty-four 8-foot panels, quite different from those being produced by Orton & Spooner, although it was still held together by ironwork and nuts and bolts with strong steel cables strained around it.

Equally, as has been mentioned, the 'Wall of Death' was far from being a universal name around this time. A postcard from 1931 shows an 'Auto Drome of Death' at the Stratford upon Avon Mop Fair, a Wall of Death in all but name with a message on the stage declaring that the riders are 'human flies cheating the undertaker'. Another features the 'Famous Hell Riders', which advertised itself as offering not only a 'thrilling race' but also 'racing lions' and 'feminine courage'. This permanent show had four riders, two from Australia, one Briton and one American who rode with the lions and first appeared at Olympia and then at Blackpool.

The name was too good not to stick though; it summed the whole act up so well, and as early as 1930 postcards show a Wall proudly proclaiming itself to be 'The Original Wall of Death', with admission set at 6d for adults and 3d for children. This Wall belonged to Tornado Smith from Boxford, Suffolk, a man who, like the American with the Hell Riders, had a thing about lions and was to go on to become one for the biggest Wall superstars of the inter-war years. Before Smith the Wall had been owned by Earl Ketring, who had brought it to the UK from his home country America. As with Winnie Souter, his early career is worth examining in detail, both for its own sake and to offer an illustration of how he and countless others found their way into this new profession.

The oldest of four boys, George Smith, as he was then, was born in 1908 at Newton Green, Sudbury. Initially a carpenter and then an AA man, Smith became a taxi driver and it was on delivering a fare in Southend in July 1929 that he first set eyes upon a Wall of Death. He was impressed by the Wall, but less so with the riders and, with the unshakeable self-confidence that was to mark his later career, he decided he

THE GLORY DAYS

Cyclone Danny, rider on the Drome of Death.

could do better himself. His break came when he answered an advertisement for an assistant working with a Wall in Whitley Bay, Newcastle, making the round trip from his parent's pub in Boxford, Suffolk in a day to apply for the job. The job involved being a mechanic and 'pushing off' the riders as they got ready to mount the Wall at the Spanish City amusement park. He got the job and before long was teaching himself how to ride the Wall, not altogether successfully at first, as he had his first crash almost immediately, significant enough to appear in the local press[15], when an eyewitness reported that Smith, not yet Tornado, had had 'a miraculous escape from death'. Some allowance may be made for exaggeration here, however, as earlier in the same report it was pointed out that no one else had been present at the crash, Smith having sneaked in to gain his experience.

Later tales of extensive treatment should also be taken with a pinch of salt, as the newspaper reported 'a wound to the forehead and abrasion of the right elbow', despite their undoubted desire to hype the incident up – Smith was reported to be travelling at an unlikely 50-60mph at the time. Smith persevered and, in September of the same year had his first public engagement in Sweden, riding for Silodromes Ltd. Riding under the name of 'Tornado' for the first time, Smith shared the billing with an American rider called Bud Leggatt and 'The Two Rosellis', known as 'The Motor Cyklist Devils'.

Smith went on to Germany, where it has been suggested he experienced the second crash in his career when a practical joker put sugar in his petrol tank, causing the engine to cut out. Whether or not there is any truth in this, Smith cropped up next in Brighton in early 1931, and it is likely that he'd spent the winter earning money from his carpentry. It was in 1931 that Smith really began to establish himself and a reputation for daring during an engagement at the Kursaal in Southend, which was to become his base. It was here that he perfected his routines of riding with his hands held in the air, controlling the bike with his knees, going round facing backwards and 'dipping and diving' a second rider round the Wall. Smith rapidly became a star, although a less-likely looking star it's difficult to imagine. With his ever-present beret and glasses, he had more of the look of Michael Crawford as the hapless Frank Spencer, and comparisons have also been made, more menacingly, to his contemporary Oswald Mosley. Such was his growing fame that part of the following winter was spent at Bertram Mills' Circus at Olympia, where he met his wife, Doris. Legend has it he took her up on the Wall on his handlebars and literally 'swept her off her feet', during which she promptly fainted.

It turned out to be a temporary aberration, as by Easter 1932 the woman who'd never ridden a motorbike before had become Smith's partner both in life and on the Wall. She had to have her own nickname of course and chose 'Dynamite Doris', a name later changed to 'Marjorie Dare'. Doris made her debut at the Barry Island amusement park dressed, like Smith, in boots, riding britches, a scarlet shirt and, naturally, a beret. The couple married in 1934 on Christmas Day, and such was their celebrity status by that time that their wedding also made the papers.

Many Wall riders have suggested that Smith was a good, but not great rider. His greatest talent lay in understanding the need for showmanship, that the paying customers parted with the cash to buy a dream or a story. Smith's special talent was to know that he couldn't afford to rest on his laurels and every new season brought a new twist to his act. The first of these was perhaps the most spectacular, the introduction of a lion bought from Chapman's Circus. Smith was playing a long game, buying the lion as a cub and training it so that it became totally familiar with the Wall. A female, Smith named his lioness Briton and trained her to ride with him on the bike. Before long she was too big, however, and had to have her own sidecar.

Having a lion wasn't a unique attraction, but it was here that Smith demonstrated his showmanship, walking the lion around the streets like a dog and finding any number of what we would today call photo opportunities to publicise his act. Summers in the mid-1930s were spent at the Kursaal and winters at his home at the White Hart, his parents' pub in the village of Boxford, where he earned some money building caravans, including his own home. This need to earn money in the winter months was common for most Wall riders, although Smith, like a few others, also managed to secure commissions abroad, riding in Sweden, Germany and Italy.

Smith's talent for self-publicity is also demonstrated by the fact that his 'family' of three was the subject of a Pathé news feature, which spread his fame across the country and secured his celebrity status. He also rode round the streets on a two-wheeled vehicle that couldn't have been further removed from his Indians, a large penny-farthing, and a later addition to his act was the so-called 'Giraffe-Necked Girl' from Burma, a girl with a ringed neck who Smith claimed to have noticed in the crowd and incorporated into his act.

THE GLORY DAYS

Signed pre-war postcard from Tornado Smith and Marjorie Dare.

Tornado Smith with Briton the lion on his sidecar.

Tornado Smith trick riding a BSA A7.

1935 became Smith's 'Year of Crashes', a period when his slogan 'Tornado Smith Rides with Death' came too close to coming true. In fact this slogan was born from another typical Smith stunt – riding round with a coffin as a sidecar, out of which a skeleton would appear at the tug of a string. Again, crashes are a way of life for most Wall riders, and often they come in bunches. Sooner or later your luck has to turn, even if you happen to be 'Tornado' Smith.

Despite being one of the features most associated with Smith, Briton was not part of the act for long, although she continued to be paraded around and used for publicity. For a while she was substituted by a small black lamb called 'Sparky', although it is unknown whether the lion ever actually lay down with the lamb. Smith regularly took his Wall back to Boxford for charity events, a gesture that made him a local hero in that village to the extent that today he is even commemorated on the village's sign. By the time war broke out Smith was the most famous Wall rider in the country and, when the Kursaal was forced to close down, he volunteered to become a fighter pilot, although he was turned down as he wore glasses. Instead he served in the Merchant Navy and became a despatch rider for the Fire Service.

THE GLORY DAYS

Above: Literally riding with death – Tornado riding with a 'pop-up' skeleton in a sidecar.

Right: Back home – Tornado performing in Boxford.

THE ORIGINAL
WALL OF DEATH
FEATURING
TORNADO SMITH
AND
MARJORIE DARE,
is open at
BOXFORD "WHITE HART"
(for one more week only), on
Wednesday 13th, Saturday 16th,
and Wednesday 20th November.
At 3.30, 7, 8, 9 and 10.   [630p

RIDING THE WALL OF DEATH

Speedy Bob Lee riding at Blackpool as one of the Wizards of the Wall.

Regrettably his marriage also broke down at this point, and Briton too died, shot by Smith when she broke a leg. He laid her to rest in an area of garden at the front of the White Hart, although this is now concreted over. A small headstone bore the inscription:

BRITON
The Wall of Death She Rode With Safety
In Her Cage She Met Her Doom

Smith may have been the most famous Wall rider, but he was far from alone. No one knows exactly how many Walls were operating in the 1930s. Estimates have varied between twenty and fifty, although a number nearer the higher end of this range seems more likely given the sheer scale of activity involving the Wall at that time. Walls were also a feature of the Oktoberfest in Munich, and have been ever since, with a photograph from 1930 showing four English riders on an American Wall, two men and two women: Crasher Evans, Speedy Bob Lee and Curly Lou Cody, fresh from his triumphs at Ramsgate, along with a fourth, unnamed rider. Although interrupted by the Second World War, there has always been a strong tradition of English riders in Germany.

Meanwhile, Germany was raising its own generation of home-grown Wall legends, including Heinz Meiners, Kitty Muller, Pitt Löffelhardt and the four Mack brothers. A one-time sewing machine mechanic, Meiners became a Wall rider when he found

Signed postcard of Speedy Curly Lee, his brother Billy Lee and Ray James.

the market too crowded in his initial chosen occupation. Starting in 1935, Meiners was to have an extraordinarily long career as a Wall rider, stretching either side of the Second World War. In 1987, at the age of seventy-five, Meiners went up one last time on a 1927 Indian Scout, still wearing the white shirt and black pullover that had become his trademark, showing all of the grace and skill that had been a hallmark of his long career, during which time he crashed around two dozen times.

Kitty Muller was already riding from the 1930 season, having learned the year before about the Wall from an English actor friend who'd visited the family. Muller has a good claim to be the first female German rider and indeed one of the first German riders of either sex, having ridden on the Wall owned by another actor, Hugo Haase, in Hamburg. From 1935 onwards she was engaged by another German legend, Pitt Löffelhardt, whose Wall she minded in Strasbourg and Metz during the subsequent war.

Initially a racing car driver, Löffelhardt himself had been riding since the early 1930s and gained a reputation for himself as a good trick rider with a good dose of showmanship thrown in. Regional newspapers at the time reported how he sat on his tank and then side saddle, moved on to kneeling on his saddle and then stretched both arms out, greeting the crowd with a broad smile before going into a routine of snake lines[16]. Löffelhardt went on to enlarge his Wall to accommodate a car and continued to take his Wall into Italy to perform in front of German troops when he could get leave after being drafted into the army.

RIDING THE WALL OF DEATH

Back home, it wasn't unknown for two or three Walls to operate at one fair, sometimes side by side and, given this level of competition, the pressure was on to be more daring and outrageous than your neighbour. In addition, there were the permanent Walls at Butlin's and venues such as Belle Vue in Manchester, Olympia in London, Merrie England in Ramsgate and of course the Kursaal, making it all the more important to come up with fresh material.

Meanwhile, the Wall of Death had proved that it was no passing fad, it was here to stay. The public remained hungry for more and more outlandish stunts. As they continued to experience hard times in their everyday lives they seemed to yearn for some kind of diversion offering a complete contrast to the daily routine. Economic conditions had, if anything, hardened during the early years of the 1930s. Unemployment peaked at just below three million in 1932 and only really stabilised, rather than improved, under the National Government formed the year before. It wasn't until midway through the decade that the number drawing the dole began to fall markedly, in part due to investment made in re-arming the country.

The proprietors and riders duly rose to the challenge to provide ever more thrills, as the exploits of Tornado Smith amply testify. Exploits included a repertoire of tricks ranging from the basic (to a Wall rider at least) stunt of riding round standing up to going round the Wall side saddle, with arms crossed and backwards, to the suicidal. Girls being plucked from the audience to ride around the Wall on the handlebars also became commonplace. Blindfolded riders became common, although Alf Miers, known as Arno, the armless rider, was out there on his own. Born without arms, Alf rode a Wall at New Brighton on the Wirral, Lancashire in 1937 owned and operated by Ken Hood, controlling the bike with his knees. He also rode a car on the Wall and was, so it is claimed, a competent mechanic, capable of stripping down an engine with his feet.

Lions have also raised their heads, quite literally, already in this story. They had been a standard part of Motordrome shows in America from the late 1920s, where they continued until after the Second World War. One particular variation of using them was the 'Liondrome', where bikes would go up on the Wall before the beasts would be released from their den under the ramp and wander around the pit, reaching up the Wall to the riders and snarling menacingly. This variation of the thrill is thought to have been the origination of the name the 'Race of Life', which later became the 'Race of Death', the traditional closing part of a Wall show.

Lions became such a feature of the Wall of Death show that they became almost commonplace. Training a lion to go up on the Wall, usually in a sidecar, was no easy matter, however, and was usually accomplished by raising a cub, with one rider designated the lion handler. Like riders, some lions were naturals and others less so. In the early 1930s Wall owner Billy Grant was trying to train a lion to go up on his Wall and getting nowhere. His team could get the lion to lie on the sidecar, but

Alf Miers, known as Arno, the armless Wall rider.

every time the engine started he'd bolt. One trainer had tried hitting it with a stick and for his troubles was prevented from ever sharing the floor of the Wall with the lion again. Eventually Billy Grant himself took charge, dosing the lion's meat with sleeping pills and getting it up on the Wall in a comatose state, gradually reducing the dose over time.

The better riders could go round backwards. Spectacular to watch, this stunt was as difficult as it looked. Not so much the sitting backwards and controlling the bike, if you got the momentum and balance right this more or less looked after itself, but actually getting there was the tough part. The rider had to literally pull their legs round against the gravitational forces, lifting the dead weight over the tank and then over the back wheel.

RIDING THE WALL OF DEATH

Jack Barry's Wall, complete with cage and lion on the front.

There are only so many tricks you can do as a rider though, and the competition was so tight that if you invented a new one that was any good the chances were your rivals would learn it before too long. Most riders stuck to a similar three-part act, probably lasting around ten minutes depending on the situation. This would nearly always end with the 'Race of Death' with up to four riders going round the track simultaneously. The room for trickery was in the middle section of the act.

If a rider was really good at something they might find it became associated with them alone, becoming their 'signature' trick. George Todd, for example, is thought to have pioneered the trick of pulling someone (actually his brother Bob) round on a pair of roller skates, something he was doing as early as 1932. These weren't conventional roller skates but had larger wheels and the act consisted of Bob holding on to a rope that span around the centre pole as he was taken up and around the Wall by a bike. When he judged the moment to be right he let go of the rope and freewheeled down like something going down a plughole. Perhaps unsurprisingly Bob wasn't that keen on the act and didn't stay with the Wall for long.

Ketring and Dare, performing at Olympia, were also among the few who could ride round in opposite directions, a trick also performed by Billy Ward and his partner as early as 1929. Most riders learn to ride anticlockwise, to go the other way round is counter-intuitive for them, the risk being compounded when there's someone coming at you from the 'right' way round.

THE GLORY DAYS

Even Tornado Smith found he was pushing the limit of the possible at times. In 1935 he introduced 'The Girl on the Flying Trapeze' with his new wife Marjorie Dare going round the Wall perched on his shoulders, using only a pair of reins to hang on. On Easter Sunday she fell when she lost her balance, landing on the ramp. She was lucky because the bike stayed on the Wall and it's when the bike falls on top of performers that the most damage is done. She suffered shock, concussion and bad bruises but in true showman style announced 'the show must go on'. Whether spurred on by Tornado or not is not known, but she didn't miss one of the hundred shows remaining and continued with an arm in a sling and bandages wrapped round her head, something that provoked cheers from the crowd every time.

What Tornado did appreciate was that it wasn't necessarily the difficulty of the trick or stunt, but how it fitted into the act. Good entertainment isn't always about doing the impossible, leaving them happy can at times mean simply surprising or amusing your audience or dazzling them. Just because something looks difficult doesn't mean it has to be difficult. He understood the basic performer's maxim of smoke and mirrors – it's not what you do, it's what it looks like that counts.

Like others, Tornado also understood the lure of animals. Along with lions, monkeys were a favourite with the Wall. In some cases these would go round with the rider, in others they would perform in their own scaled down 'Monkey Drome' on their own bikes, an act presented by Arthur 'Ace' Hadley and Jack North in the early 1930s. Others coped with the competition by taking their acts on tour abroad. Walls were loaded onto ships and taken not only to Germany but countries such as Sweden, South Africa and China, with home-grown Walls appearing in France and the Netherlands. Some of these included the American pioneers who had come over at the end of the 1920s and had been squeezed out by English riders, including Bob Carew, one of the first to come to England.

After conquering England, Carew and his fellow riders, Robby Hayhurst and the woman rider Kitty O'Neill, had gone on to tour most of Europe. In 1936 they decided to chance their luck in Russia and spent two seasons there. Conscious that the international situation was darkening, they decided to leave and the Russian government was happy to let them go – so long as they left their (by now two) Walls behind. It seems they'd liked the show so much they wanted to hang onto it. Hayhurst made it back via Poland and gave up the Wall of Death to make a living from solo trick riding, including an act that involved standing at the top of a 9-foot ladder balanced on his Indian while he revolved round a 13-foot radius stage.

One of these Walls was completely restored after the war in Russia with new chrome added and the original eighteen wooden panels replaced by steel. The other turned up in South Africa in the mid-1990s complete with building instructions translated into Russian on the side. After being 'requisitioned' this had subsequently toured the

Above: Ketring and Dare at Olympia, in 1930-31, showing their dexterity by having two bikes going in opposite directions, a rarely attempted feat.

Above left: A 'Monkeydrome' next to a Wall – 'Monkeys operate their own machines.'

Left: A monkey riding a bike in Sydney, Australia.

motherland and, after the war, countries behind the Iron Curtain, until those operating it could no longer afford to run it and it was left to rot, later finding its way to South Africa in two giant trailers. Once discovered it was shipped to Holland and re-erected and a Dutch rider was located to ride it. This Wall continues to perform periodically in Europe to this day.

That this Wall was in such good condition is a testament to the workmen who'd built it nearly three-quarters of a century before. Equally impressive is the lasting nature of the attraction of the Wall as entertainment, which has endured just as long. Part of this can be put down to another part of the act that had proved itself over time – the machine, specifically the Indian motorcycles, still the bike of choice for Wall riders today despite looking like a museum piece. Another factor driving the Wall of Death's longevity has been the ingenuity of those presenting the act. Some examples of this have already been cited, but the coming of another war is a good place to pause and consider this combination of machines and ingenuity in greater detail.

FOUR

GOING ROUND

Going round a Wall of Death naturally requires a bike and, for most Wall riders, one bike in particular stands out. Its very appearance suggests that it has stood the test of time, but much more than that, it's proven itself in the school of experience over eight decades.

Given the Wall's reputation for showmanship and hyperbole, it is perhaps a surprising choice. Skeletal in appearance, and lacking any of the features of the sort of high-powered road machine usually favoured by hardcore bikers, it looks more like a museum piece than the sort of machine you'd risk your neck on, day in day out, on the Wall, and in many ways that's where it should be. Usually painted red, often by hand with the brush strokes still visible close up, this singular bike is the 1920s Indian Scout.

Manufactured by the Hendee Manufacturing Co. of Springfield, Massachusetts, later to become the Indian Motorcycle Co., the company went out of business over fifty years ago in 1953, but their Indians live on. The name Indian was chosen deliberately to convey a sense of America and freedom by the company's two founders, both of whom were from European stock, respectively Spanish and Swedish. This may go some way to help explaining the bikes' enduring attraction to subsequent generations of European riders; that and an early policy by the company in favour of export. The bikes were promoted under the slogan, 'You can't wear out an Indian Scout', a boast that Wall riders were to verify over subsequent generations.

In the early and glory days of the Wall Scouts were so popular that riders were known to have chased after machines they spotted on the road and offer to buy them off the unsuspecting owner. So what was it about the Indians that made them so special? Manufactured from 1920, Scouts were 600cc 42°V-twin cylinder machines with a left-handed foot-operated clutch and a three-speed hand-shift gearbox. Uniquely, the bike combined a number of critical features together into one bike, almost as if, according

Indians endorsed by a Wall Show – note the small child at the front.

to some riders, it was designed specially to be used on a Wall. Another group of riders who favoured Scouts were US police departments during the Prohibition era. Like the Wall riders that followed, who went round their Walls counter-clockwise, they particularly appreciated the left-hand throttle, although in their case this was because this allowed them to draw their gun with their right hand and keep motoring.

For Wall riders there was much more to Scouts than the position of their throttle. The machines had a low centre of gravity and a short wheelbase, with the big twin-cylinder engine producing power low down, where it was needed. The bikes also had no rear suspension and a front leaf spring, which together meant the machine was virtually rigid, which was exactly what a rider needs on a Wall. The front leaf also gives the rider somewhere to put his foot when trick riding. The stable ride also makes it easier for the rider to let go of the handlebars.

Other features that endear the bike to Wall riders include the fact that the throttle cables pass inside the handlebars, making a 'snag' much less likely when moving around on the machine. Furthermore, on the earlier bikes at least, the handlebars, saddle and tank were all at the same height, making it easier to move between them when performing stunts.

GOING ROUND

The tank itself also has a frame tube over it, so most trick riders liked to pad it, using some carpet felt with a groove down the middle that they then covered with leather, so they could slide up the tank from the seat in a smooth motion under pressure from the G-force. Another stunt-friendly feature is the bike's footboards in place of the more usual pegs, which make standing up easier, especially if a rider wants to put both feet on the same side. Finally, the bike's lubrication system means that it doesn't leave much oil on the wooden side of the Wall – an absolutely critical consideration for any Wall rider – and its trailing link front fork gives it particularly good steering.

Not that Wall riders use factory-standard machines. Like modern racers, they each have their own quirks and preferences, effectively customizing a bike to their own specifications. Some go as far as actually to shorten the frame, reducing the wheelbase, and most will pay some attention to the forks by way of insurance against a break when they're up on the Wall. One piece of attention most pay is to hit them with a sledgehammer cushioned with a block of wood in order to bend the forks into the desired angle so the bikes stay up when riding with no hands, although this rendered them useless for anything other than Wall riding. On-the-road bikes also have sprung saddles, but these are replaced with solid metal struts for the Wall. Likewise, the exhaust system is replaced with two short stub pipes.

An Indian in action on the Wall, ridden by Allan Ford.

RIDING THE WALL OF DEATH

Indians used on Messham's show. The one on the far right is the roller bike while the others are all trick bikes.

Everything that can go, does go. Mudguards, speedometers, headlights and anything else that would make the bike recognisable as a road machine is stripped off, which in part accounts for the bike's skeletal appearance – although most riders like to keep a short piece of mudguard just in case they should slip back onto the rear tyre. The one addition riders usually liked to install was a cut-out button on the right, often made out of a piece of hacksaw blade and insulating tape, allowing the rider to make the bike bang and crack as it goes round the Wall – anything to add to the show.

The tyres are also an object of much attention. Friction from the rubber on the tyres, along with centrifugal force, is what keeps the bike 'stuck' to the Wall and, as such, their condition is vital. Despite appearances, bikes don't go round the Wall at ninety degrees; it just looks that way when you're looking up or down on them. As such, the tyres meet the Wall at an angle and different riders, depending upon the speed they like to travel at, the tricks they perform and their own height and weight, prefer different 'slopes' on their tyres. On a fresh tyre this can mean going so far as to take a surform tool to the rubber and planing the tyre down to the required angle. Over the course of a season riders look to maintain this angle, turning the tyre round and starting again once the canvas starts to appear. Another way of maintaining the angle for as long as possible required the use of washers, swapping them over from one side to the other as the tyre wears. Tyre pressures are also important. The rider's aim is for stability not a smooth ride; a 300-pound machine would be pumped up to 40psi, whereas an 800-pound road machine might only have 50psi.

GOING ROUND

Indians weren't the only way to go round a Wall; it's possible to take most machines up but if you're riding the Wall every day you get to value reliability above all else. Tornado Smith once told a story[17] of how three local motorcycle enthusiasts wanted proof that an ordinary road machine could go up the Wall and got permission to test their own bikes on his Wall. Having failed miserably, they declared that Tornado was using some kind of trickery, whereupon he took each of their bikes, in turn a 550cc Triumph, a 346cc Royal Enfield and a 349cc James, up what he liked to call the 'perp' or perpendicular.

After the Second World War Indian parts became increasingly hard to come by and other makes became more common. With the cessation of hostilities, Tornado Smith was one of the first to get a Wall up and running again, by which time he'd moved on to using BSA 500cc A7s. These had the distinction of being the only bikes ever specially manufactured for Wall riding, with BSA using the last of their rigid frames to make them, although they were adapted by adding a footrest where the front spring would have been on an Indian to make it easier to stunt ride. BSAs were favoured by many riders through the 1950s and 1960s and, although they were cheaper to run than an Indian, they were also much heavier, causing the Wall itself to sway in an at times alarming way during the Race of Death at the end of a show.

The Indian footrest – one of the features that made it attractive to Wall riders.

RIDING THE WALL OF DEATH

Gustav Kokos working on one of the original factory-supplied Tornado Smith BSAs.

A pair of BMWs waiting on the floor at the Oktoberfest in Munich. (Courtesy Neil Smart)

GOING ROUND

In a homage to Smith, Wall rider Allan Ford built a pair of replica BSAs in the 1980s. Although an Indian devotee, Ford also built a couple of BSA 175 Bantams with D1 rigid frames as teaching machines. At this time, before the market became flooded with Japanese bikes, Bantams were plentiful and Indians too precious to be risked with trainees. They were light, had the right power and, most important of all, they worked. One bike rejected by most riders were Triumphs – they simply leaked too much oil. Once the Japanese had become dominant Allan Ford also used Honda CD200s, which had the three virtues of good gearing, reliability and cheapness. Harley Davidsons have also been used on Walls, but this tends to be an American phenomenon; as have BMWs, again, as might be expected, mainly in Germany. Incredibly, even Lambretta scooters have featured on the Wall. In 1961 a reporter with *Motor Cycling* magazine[18] went up Tornado Smith's Wall in Southend on a Lambretta, although the sight of a scooter on Smith's 'perp' seems to go against the grain a little, and standard TV175 Lambrettas were also a regular feature on a 16.5-foot high Swiss Wall in the mid-1960s.

In 2005 Wall Rider Ken Fox even managed to take a steam-powered bike up on his wall[19]. Following a challenge issued by the West of England Steam Engine Society, who put up a £1,000 prize, steam car enthusiast Gerry Stoneman from Devon offered an adapted 1920 Field steam-powered motorcycle that Ken, having tested it beforehand, duly took up on his Wall. The machine was petrol fired and would not run on the Wall with its burner alight. As a result the run up the Wall had to be made with a stored head of steam. Proof, if proof were needed, that practically any bike can go up on the Wall in the right hands.

Bikes, whatever their make, lie at the heart of a Wall of Death show. They tap into the free spirit, the idea of the last frontier, the defiance of danger, the fascination with, and proximity to, death. They are not the only vehicles that have been seen going round a Wall though. A logical addition in the 1930s was the sidecar, which were growing in popularity on the road. Used on the Wall, they opened up a whole fresh arena of stunt opportunities. As ever, the ultimate showman Tornado Smith was quick to get in on the act, and we have seen how he used his sidecar as a means of bringing his lion up onto the Wall rather than simply circling below in the pit as had been the tradition up until that point, and it has also been noted how he used one to carry a skeleton in a coffin-shaped sidecar operated by a spring.

Getting a sidecar up onto the Wall can be tricky and, in contrast to the tendency to make everything on the bike as rigid as possible, the tubes linking the bike to the sidecar have to be hinged to provide the necessary 'give' to make the transition from the ramp to the Wall. Equally, for a brief while, the rider finds themselves in two dimensions, on the Wall on the bike, but on the ramp with the sidecar. This requires special expertise to handle and feels awkward although, in Germany, where sidecars

RIDING THE WALL OF DEATH

Honda and sidecar at the Oktoberfest in Munich. (Courtesy Neil Smart)

have proved especially durable as an attraction, the bike and sidecar are the other way round, which added to the difficulty for British riders plying their trade at the many fairs in that country.

From sidecars to small cars, the leap was perhaps inevitable. Many have claimed to be the first to take a car up on the Wall, but perhaps the only fact we can be certain of is that Tornado Smith was not the first to manage this feat, which he achieved in 1934/35, despite his own claims to the contrary. That many remember him as the first is perhaps more a testament to his own talent for self-publicity, as he wrote extensively about his experiences in *The Austin* magazine in May of 1935 in which he described how he adapted a standard road model of an Austin Seven, which he says he selected from twenty British and foreign cars due to its strong structure and light weight.

One car pioneer was called Smith, not Tornado but a twenty-five-year-old speedway rider called Brisbane Smith who gave up dirt-track racing to take up the Wall of Death. Brisbane had toured in the UK with Stutz's World Fair in 1930, earning a reputation for being particularly fearless. Determined to be the first to go round in a car he too selected an Austin Seven and started practising.

GOING ROUND

Although undoubtedly brave, Brisbane suffered from the worst vice a trainee can possess: impatience. While perfecting his act before an evening show at Poole Fair in late 1931, he took the car to the top of the Wall and hit the safety cable. The Austin fell and Brisbane fell with it, with the car unfortunately just coming second, burying the driver. Brisbane died shortly afterwards in hospital of horrific injuries. The Wall of Death had been bloodied and finally earned its sobriquet. To Brisbane went the dubious honour of being its first victim, although perhaps ironically it was a car, not a bike, that conferred this title on him.

Postcard evidence exists of cars going round the Wall from as early as the 1930/31 season, with early pioneers Ketring and Patsie Dare, mentioned in the previous chapter for riding in opposite directions, having a good claim for being among the first. Photographic evidence also exists of Dare Devil Alma Skinner and Speedy Rube going round a Wall in a car in Scarborough in 1932, with one photo showing a seemingly posed car crash and another showing them posing in front of their show against a banner proclaiming 'Now Featuring Racing Car on the Wall'.

Similarly, records show a car going round a Wall in Bucharest, Romania in May 1934. More tellingly perhaps, another postcard marked as 1928, but probably 1929, shows Pat Collins' Death Riders at Manchester's Belle Vue posing with bikes and a car. It is worth noting, though, that posters around the riders in the postcard mention only the bikes, so the car may have been there simply to draw the public in.

Up on the 'perp', Tornado Smith in an Austin 7.

RIDING THE WALL OF DEATH

Cars soon appeared on the Wall, but it was the bikes that really thrilled.

KETRING & PATSIE DARE.—Olympia, 1930-31.

Ketring and Dare were also noteworthy for being two of the first to go around the Wall in a car, again at Olympia.

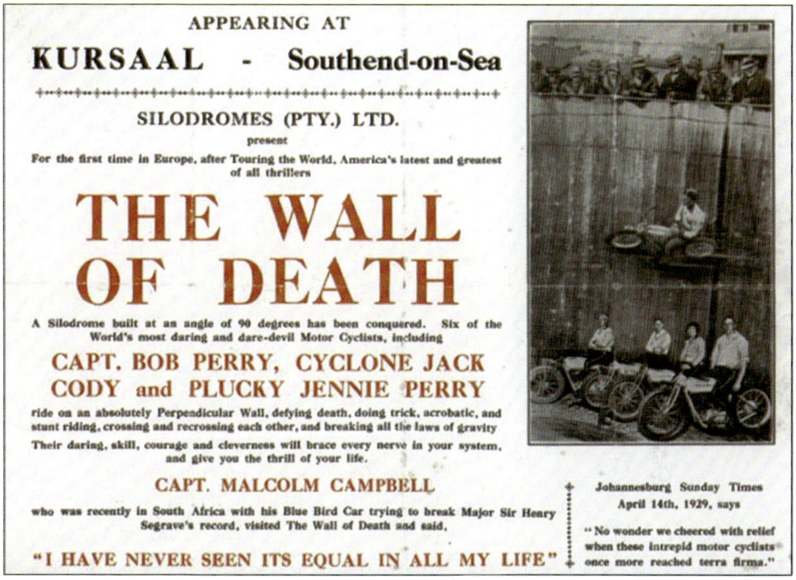

1. One of the earliest mentions of the Wall, featuring Bob Perry, Jack Cody and Jennie Perry at the Kursaal in 1929, including a quote from Malcolm Campbell.

2. Doug Murphy's Indian, on which he rode all over the world.

3. A typical Indian as used on the Wall.

4. A pair of Indians on the front of the Motordrome Company show.

5. The bike built by Sergei Chityan in Russia especially for the Wall of Death.

6. Allan Ford taking a go-kart round the Wall.

7. Evidence of how much easier it was to transport a Globe than a Wall.

8. *Above left:* The Varanne brothers, Globe and Wall riders, although the Globe is their speciality.

9. *Above right:* Charles Winter with Doug Mac Valley while riding in the US. (Copyright Charles Winter)

10. *Left:* Yvonne Stagg's Wall (ex-Tornado Smith) in the Kursaal, mid-1960s.

11. *Below:* The front of Tommy Messham's show when it was the last travelling one around. (Copyright Charles Winter)

12. The Iranian Wall ridden by Allan Ford in the 1980s.

13. Sergei Chityan riding the Wall he built himself. Note the lack of tilt.

14. A rickety Wall in India, complete with bicycle. (Courtesy Neil Smart)

15. Not all Walls necessarily reach the highest health and safety standards – a Wall in India in the 1990s. (Courtesy Neil Smart)

16. Dabbert's Wall in Germany.

17. Inside Dabbert's Wall in Germany, complete with racing car.

18. A Wall of Death in Holland, 1988.

19. The Wall arriving on a ground, ready to be built up.

20. The Build (1) – laying out the sleepers on the packing, centre already in place.

21. The Build (2) – the floor down.

22. The Build (3)
– erecting the panels.

23. The Build (4)
– walkrounds and handrails up.

24. The Build (5)
– nearly finished, just the front to build up.

25. The worst build-up ever! Norwich, Christmas Fair, Tommy Messham's Wall, early 1970s.

26. Sprucing up before a show – Ken Wolf, Gerry de Roy and Chris Lee.

27. *Above:* Showtime!

28. *Right:* Ned Kelly demonstrating his dexterity on the rollers, Pitt's Wall, Germany. (Courtesy Neil Smart)

29. James Messham's Wall at Shoreham Air Show, 2005.

30. Allan Ford's (ex-Albert Evans) Wall rotting away at Harris' yard at Ashington.

31. *Eat the Peach* – sold on the line that 'All they ever wanted to do was ride high.'

32. *Above left:* Charles Winter and actor Stephen Brennan in front of the Wall built for *Eat the Peach*. (Copyright Charles Winter)

33. *Above right:* Filming inside the Wall for *Eat the Peach*. Note the bike attached to an arm revolving around the centre pole. (Copyright Charles Winter)

34. *Above:* Castrol poster featuring Yvonne Stagg riding.

35. *Left:* Signed poster advertising Lucky Thibeault's show in the US, 1990. (Courtesy Charles Winter)

36. *Above left:* Poster advertising the French Varanne brothers and their 'Mur de la Mort', 1990.

37. *Above right:* A poster advertising the 1930 Oktoberfest featuring a Wall of Death.

38. *Right:* A comic book featuring the Wall of Death.

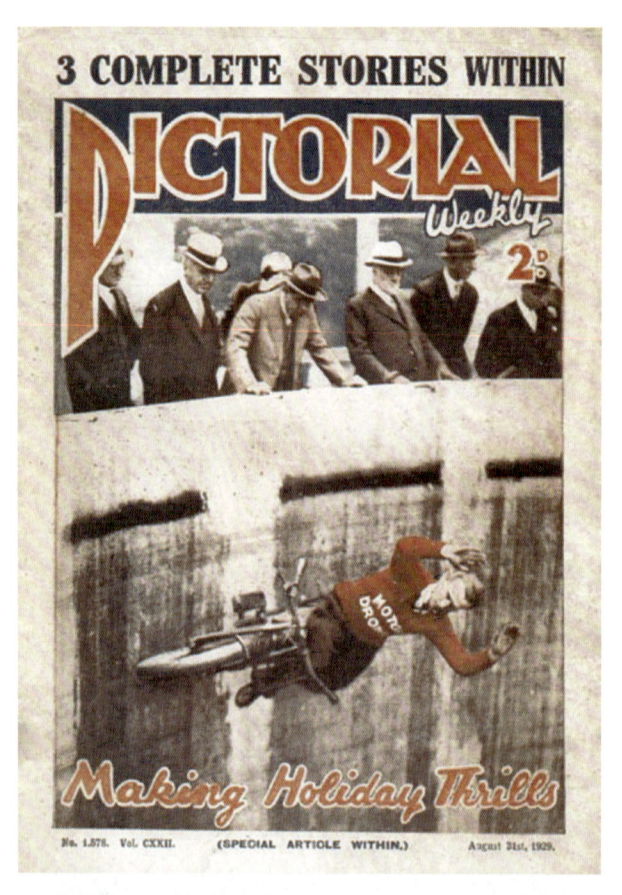

39. An early reference to the Wall, in the *Weekly Pictorial*, August 1929.

40. Cover of the *Wizard* annual 1948, showing how the Wall had entered the public consciousness.

GOING ROUND

Doug Murphy on a go-kart at the Oktoberfest 1961 – even wearing a tie!

Although popular for a while, cars didn't seem to capture the true spirit of the Wall. Going round in a car was impressive but left little room for trickery and showmanship, and it was this, combined with the greater danger riding a bike seemed to represent, that the crowds were prepared to pay for. From a practical point of view, cars were also a problem in that they were too large to go through the door and, as such, Walls had to be built up round them. This also limited the room for manoeuvre if they needed any work done on them. The spirit of going round on four wheels was later captured through the use of go-karts, although these came to the fore after the Second World War and still continue today, offering a better mix of novelty and vulnerability.

So long as there was competition between Walls the need for novelty was always there, and proprietors and riders alike have shown remarkable imagination over the years to make sure their act was just that little bit different. Sidecars, cars, karts and roller skates all offered their own attraction. Likewise, there have even been attempts to take the Wall back to its roots and reintroduce cyclists on the Wall. When boiled down, though, what the public really appreciated was the noise, vibration, smell and sheer thrill offered by motorbikes, and it is these that have remained at the heart of the Wall of Death show.

So what does it actually feel like to be going round a Wall on two wheels at speeds in excess of 40mph? Hundreds have experienced this thrill for themselves, some as

One of the first cars on the Wall – appearing on the Todd brothers' wall at Merrie England in Ramsgate in 1932.

A rare example of roller skating around a Wall, at Merrie England in Ramsgate in 1932, featuring Bob Todd on the skates.

professionals, some as trainees and others on a one-off basis. For the professionals the art of riding a Wall becomes second nature and many have gone on to ride for decades. Like learning to swim, it is something you never forget and for some it becomes a bug they can never get out of their system. Serious trick riders have to learn their art, and few graduate onto tricks before they have earned their spurs putting in the hours going round the Wall show after show, day after day, week after week for around a year. It takes this long to learn to respect the Wall, to have experienced most things that can go wrong, to learn to become one with your machine, understand its foibles and generate a sixth sense around the forces that are keeping you pinned to the wooden circle. It probably also helps to take a couple of spills and to learn the virtue of patience. Any seasoned rider will tell you that it's the riders who try to go too far too fast that don't make it.

So how do you get started? Perhaps the biggest surprise awaiting a novice rider is that despite the act's obvious danger no one wears a helmet. The centrifugal forces

GOING ROUND

make this highly uncomfortable; it would be like going round with a bowling ball on your shoulders. If someone is serious about becoming a Wall rider, and the owner of the Wall is prepared to let them try, the first step is to find a space in between shows and clear the Wall so that it's empty. The lesson starts by simply getting the new rider used to going round and round the floor and then up onto the banking. There's no practising outside the Wall first, it's a case of cutting straight to the chase. The greatest enemy at this stage is dizziness and it is likely to take a while for the middle ear to get used to this new, unnatural, sensation. After a few laps the trainer will call the new rider to stop and rush to grab them. Without fail the novice will get off their bike and not know where they are, invariably finding their knees have decided to desert them.

This process continues in lots of short bursts punctuated by cups of tea. The aim at this stage is to build confidence and to instil the 'feel' of going round on the banking, as well as acclimatising the body to going round. Trainees also need to master the art of coming on and off the banking. In more modern times these first trips round the Wall might be done in a kart, taking away the need to maintain balance. Perhaps ironically, experienced riders will confirm that going round on the banking is actually harder than going round the Wall; you're neither in one environment nor the other and it's also more bumpy, but this is where you have to start.

This process continues until the trainer feels the new rider is ready to go up onto the Wall. This moment arrives when the rider has got the hang of the right speed and is confident riding along the 'crack' between the ramping and the Wall and may come as soon as the second or third day, depending on how much spare time the trainer has been able to find. A novice rider was taught to go round a Wall in under a week for the Noel Edmunds TV show in the 1980s for example, although this involved a very intensive schedule.

Actually mounting the Wall is achieved by flicking the wheel onto the straight surface. If the speed is right and the confidence is there, the rider finds themselves going round. At this stage what happens nine times out of ten is the rider tries to flatten themselves against the Wall, it being a natural instinct to straighten up. This inevitably results in a spill, and the rider's first hard lesson. Next time they'll know to keep their head down as if they are going round a bend, which of course they are. The new rider soon learns that centrifugal force is their friend, pinning them to the Wall at somewhere between 3 and 4G. It can also work against you though, making the machine heavier and life harder. The trick, therefore, is to manage to hit the right balance between speed, where centrifugal force works for you, and balance.

The faster you go the greater the force and the harder work it becomes, the slower you go the more the friction of the rubber of the tyres on the wood of the Wall comes into play. The experienced rider will aim to get the tyres to do

RIDING THE WALL OF DEATH

Allan Ford preparing to ride a bicycle on the Wall.

A go-kart specially made for Peter Catchpole for the Wall with a hinging rear end.

GOING ROUND

more of the work, not least because doing dozens of shows a day will become exhausting if you rely simply on speed to keep you up. Speed is also inadvisable when it comes to trick riding, as your limbs become leaden and slow to react as the gravitational force increases. As has already been highlighted, moving your leg over or up the tank requires it to be physically lifted in order to move, although this is a long way into the future for the trainee rider.

Very quickly the novice learns the basics. Riding the Wall is like tightrope walking; there's no particular black art, no magic or magnets. It's largely about confidence and having the determination to succeed. You don't have to be an experienced rider to go round a Wall, in fact some trainers prefer those who haven't ridden before as they come without preconceptions, or some kind of stunt expert; it needs some skill, a measure of determination and a generous portion of raw guts.

If the trainee is looking to become a professional, and many at this point may have proved something to themselves and decide to move on, the next step on the process is to start learning their showmanship – this is an act after all. They therefore become the first rider on in a show, absorbing the atmosphere and tension in the crowd, getting used to the buzz and the spiel and the vital importance of playing to the crowd. A trainee could be a natural on the Wall, but if they're afraid of performing in public then they're no use to anyone. A common trick used by proprietors was often to introduce a new rider as someone local they've been training up and to suggest that this is their first time on the Wall. This takes some of the pressure off the rider and adds to the interest for the crowd – whether or not they happen to be local. Their apprenticeship has begun. The next gaff might be a busy one or the Wall might not be able to pull on until the Friday if it's a big Guild show. There's no time for trainees when experienced riders are trying to cram in four or maybe even five shows an hour. At this stage they still haven't been trusted with an Indian. They are much too valuable, but they are learning their art. What follows is practice, practice, practice until they learn to live and breathe the Wall.

In time, the new rider learns to take in their surroundings. What they see is less of a blur and they may even begin to pick out individual faces in the crowd, making it easier to play to them. At some point they are also introduced onto the rollers out front, exposing them to another vital aspect of the act. Although this might look easy it isn't, more riders fall off the rollers than fall off the Wall. Experienced riders learn to make it look even harder than it is, wobbling deliberately to raise the tension.

Having a novice as the first act also helps to accentuate the thrills of those who follow. The next rider will do a straight ride performing the 'dips and dives' of death, pressing his cut-out every now and then to raise the sense of danger and aiming their bike up the Wall towards someone they've spotted in the crowd, pulling away just before they reach the safety cable. A go-kart act might follow, along with whatever

Above: Allan Ford riding without hands and feet.

Left: Chris Lee, one of the best trick riders still performing today.

tricks each of the other riders has in their repertoire, but the show will always end with the 'Race of Death' or 'Hell Riders Race' – with two, three or even at times four riders going round the Wall together. This is one of the hardest things for a new rider to learn and requires them to gain some kind of appreciation of where other riders are on the track with them – something that doesn't come easily. Furthermore, they have to learn how to go at exactly the same speed as their colleagues. Typically, the novice relies on their more experienced colleagues to ride round them in what is a highly choreographed set of manoeuvres, planned down to the last lap.

Being a trick rider or performing the 'Race of Death' means you've made it as a straight rider. But what does it feel like to go round the Wall as an ordinary member

GOING ROUND

Ned Kelly and Ken Fox going round on Honda CB200s.

of the public? These days such outings are the exception, done as part of a publicity stunt or maybe a charity special. At one time they were much more common, especially at motorbike rallies, with a favourite trick being pulling a pretty girl out of the crowd to ride on the handlebars. Modern day rider Ken Fox recalls how one of his worst crashes occurred when one such passenger decided the time was right to pull off her top and reveal the effect of gravity on her chest, completely upsetting his balance and causing him to land with a thump.

RIDING THE WALL OF DEATH

Which brings us onto the subject of accidents. These do happen of course, but only very rarely are they fatal. Even 'going over the top' needn't necessarily mean a call to the undertakers. George Todd once told the tale of how he was teaching a rider called Freddie Lee to conquer the Wall, but although he could reach the necessary speed on the banking he couldn't quite get the bike up onto the Wall. George devised a strategy of getting some of Freddie's girlfriends to watch from the walkrounds and taunt him. His pride suitably shaken, Freddie got on a bike, went straight up the Wall and over the top and out. On landing Lee picked himself up, walked up the steps and surveyed the damage.

He was lucky. Most serious injuries take place when a bike falls on the rider inside a Wall; somehow it always manages to find the rider when it comes to ground. A number of things could make this happen, the most common being a blow out, something the rider had very little control over. Other times it might have been mist on the Wall, especially where the show was on a coastal site where sand could be another hazard. Occasionally some idiot would have the bright idea of pouring beer down the side of a Wall and if glass was thrown in the rider had no option but to keep going round the Wall until it had been swept up. Another favourite was a recently-won goldfish, including its water.

Accidents were both a professional and personal disaster. Although the paying public may have subconsciously be paying to see someone hurt themselves, nothing cleared a walkround quicker than the sight of blood. Splinters were an occupational hazard, Allan Ford is often quoted as saying he carried samples of his Wall around inside him, although wood burns were more significant – riders rarely fell straight down, they usually slid down. More basically, piles were another problem, the result of spending too much time sitting round on bikes. Piles combined with toothache was said to be the Wall rider's nightmare. More than that, accidents and the injuries that come with them were an inconvenience. In good show business fashion, the show had to go on and most riders will testify to the number of times they've ridden with broken ribs or ankles splintered with spare bits of wood. Eventually more chronic conditions such as loss of hearing or varicose veins, or in extreme cases emphysema, would often curtail a riding career.

No rider means no show and in the past riders were often pulled out of Accident and Emergency waiting rooms to finish a show. Chris Lee, who started riding in the 1970s for Tommy Messham, tells how he was taken to hospital after a bad fall with a badly damaged finger dangling from his hand and was made to wait. After about an hour Messham turned up to see if he'd been seen to yet and when told he hadn't demanded Lee return to the show and get treated later.

More deaths have taken place building up or taking down a Wall than riding. One particularly nasty incident involved Len Parker, a Wall owner and rider, who

GOING ROUND

A young Tommy Messham jnr and Chris Lee both on Honda CD175s. (Copyright Charles Winter)

was killed when he left three panels standing with only one gate holding them. A sudden gust of wind caught the panels and squashed him, killing him instantly. This was not an isolated occurrence, although such deaths, more usually involving gaff lads rather than riders, cannot be described as common.

For the professional staying on the Wall requires sustained concentration. Accidents on the Wall usually occur when that concentration lapses, if the rider starts to push the limit of what they know is sensible or is simply exhausted. Post-war rider Albert Evans' most spectacular accident happened when he was trying to improve upon his trick of dislodging a five pound note draped over the safety wire. He'd managed to achieve this with his front wheel but wanted to show he could also do it with his rear. When he tried it he found himself plunging straight down the Wall, unable to control the inevitable. Later on in hospital, just after his father had asked if he was ready to finish the show, Albert was told how he looked like a 'big black bird trying to fly' as he'd hurtled through the air. He was lucky to get away with several stitches to his chin and nothing more serious. Modern-day rider Ken Fox has a good rule – he never rides outside a show, suggesting that it's when you start to show off or impress that something goes wrong. Sound advice, but perhaps less easy to accept if you haven't got decades of experience under your belt.

For amateurs, those who get involved in a one-off ride, the moral is simple – leave the showmanship to the professionals. All that's required is to do as you're told, typically to trust the rider, lean back into them and not to move an inch – and to have the willingness to go through with it. Typically, such 'passengers' tend to arrive back on solid earth spinning, but having experienced an adrenaline rush the like of which they've never had before. What's more, most of them say they'd go round again!

FIVE

THE GLOBE

There's more than one way to go round in circles on a motorbike. In terms of its pedigree, the Globe of Death stretches back just as far, if not further than the Wall, and has strong claims to be a more direct descendent of the Jones-Hilliard Bicycle Sensation and the acts performed by the likes of the Tom Davis and Hall & Wilson Trios nearly a hundred years ago.

What's more, as has already been noted, its advocates, including many of the more experienced riders, would suggest that the Globe is both more dangerous, more exciting and more challenging than the Wall. Rather than simply going round in two dimensions, riders in the Globe take in three, passing up, down and over each other and their audiences. Why then was it that the Globe failed to fix itself so firmly into the fairground scene and the public psyche? Today most people over a certain age will recognise a Wall of Death, but far fewer will ever have seen a Globe.

As we have seen, the idea of a Bowl of Death, or some kind of open metal latticework structure, be it an actual bowl, cup or saucer in which tricks were performed on motorbikes, had been around for some time before the advent of the Silodrome at the end of the 1920s. Photographic evidence exists of Globes as we would recognise them now existing as early as 1922, transported around the country on decommissioned ex-army trucks, and anecdotal evidence supports the fact that a handful of Globes were around at this time. Albert Evans senior had a Globe in the early 1920s with Albert Sedgewick, teaching themselves to ride it when the French pair of riders showed themselves to be more interested in stunt riding on a nearby beach. Evans and Sedgewick practiced at night until they were good enough to perform the act themselves, changing the padlock on the Globe so they could take it over.

The 'Death Ring' that featured at the British Empire Exhibition in 1924 is another good example, although this particular act also offers a good illustration of how such attractions tended to exist as one-offs rather than part of the mainstream scene. Part of the reason for this may have been the difficulty of erecting and transporting such a show, although this was a problem the Tom Davis Trio seemed to overcome much earlier. If so, it is understandable that one reaction to this was to make the attraction more manageable by closing off the previously open ends of the bowl or saucer and take it to what was perhaps its inevitable conclusion by making it an enclosed sphere.

While this might have been logical on a practical level, it had the effect of radically changing the nature of the attraction. Not only did it become much smaller, typically around five metres in diameter, but it became harder for the paying public to see the show, with the wire mesh necessarily obscuring the view. Whereas before this development part of the thrill of watching was the possibility that the riders might fall out of their enclosure, with the seeming magic of centrifugal forces so clearly exploited later on by the Silodromes a key ingredient, this possibility was removed when the bowl became totally enclosed. Erroneously, it made the Globe seem somehow safer, and therefore less of a thrill, an impression reinforced by the fact that riders often wore helmets and full leathers.

The evolution of Death Ring-type acts and the arrival of Globes from mainland Europe seemed to happen in tandem, causing their number to rise. Once again, in the absence of any formal records, correspondence in *World's Fair* is perhaps the best source of information on this attraction. Taking into account the need for caution with dates, bearing in mind that correspondents were writing fifty years after the events they were describing, a spate of letters in the mid-1970s in this journal suggested that Globes were seen at York's Martinmas Fairs in the period 1926-28 and also at Dorking in 1927[20].

A more detailed letter from slightly earlier[21] remembers a French Globe ridden by the Abbins brothers, one of whom, Paul, owned the act, who may or may not have been the same French duo who Albert Evans had locked out of his Globe earlier. This was being toured by 'Walsall' John Collins in the 1920s, with venues including the Hanley Wakes and Marlborough Mop Fair. The act involved a motorbike and a bicycle, with the former looping the interior of the Globe while the latter rode around at the bottom. Before the show began, in a typically flamboyant French gesture, the motorcyclist would kiss his lady in a theatrical way, as if to imply he might not come back.

While it was undoubtedly more dangerous to ride a Globe than a Wall, to the layman at least it was less of a spectacle. Not only was it less accessible, but it lost both the physical and psychological 'edge' that had been a central part of the appeal of its predecessors, and this must provide part of the explanation for its failure to take off in quite the same way that the Wall did later. Equally, with the act partially hidden behind the mesh, the paying public were also denied much of the sense of movement that made similar acts so appealing.

The Globe still offered thrills and had the combination of noise, smell, movement and danger that was to make the Silodrome so compelling an attraction, and for some time this was enough to ensure its survival. For many years from the late 1920s the Globe and Wall existed side by side, with riders such as Billy Bellhouse from Sheffield switching from one to the other and proprietors such as Silodromes Pty and Pat Collins hedging their bets on which would prove more popular in the long run by presenting both.

It has been suggested in these pages that the Globe was more of a European phenomenon, while the ancestry of the Wall lay more across the Atlantic. It is perhaps surprising therefore to find the first formal record of a complete Globe lying on the shelves of the US Patent Office. Like similar Edwardian patents in Britain for static amusements, this was intended for use with bicycles, but other than that it is an almost exact representation of the later Globe. Filed by Arthur Rosenthal from Grand Rapids in Michigan in May 1904, the invention was called the Bicyclist's Globe and put itself forward as an improvement on existing Globes, or 'bicycle whirls'.

Key features of Rosenthal's Globe were the provision of a latticed globe designed to allow 'the bicyclist to attain sufficient momentum and have sufficient structure so that he may ride beyond the vertical centre until he assumes nearly an inverted position upon his wheels'[22]. Two other improvements offered by the new invention were the development of sufficient rigidity in the structure to withstand the centrifugal force the cyclist would exert upon it and, significantly, a construct that made it easier to assemble and take the Globe apart again.

The contraption was made out of steel ribs with a band of iron around the edge and was built in sections. Another interesting feature of this Globe was the special attention Rosenthal paid to the construction of its upper half with the aim of making it easier for the audience to look in, the Globe being divided into two hemispheres, with the upper hemisphere having a minimum of obstructions.

No further evidence has come to light to reveal what became of Rosenthal's device. Perhaps, like so many in that inventive time, it came to nought, but on the other hand the idea of a globe or sphere had clearly embedded itself in the public consciousness. A report in the US publication *The Motocycle News*[23] dated April 1909 features a photograph of woman called C'Dora who was said to 'loop "The Globe of Death"'. Usefully, this is accompanied by a photograph showing the lady in question riding upside down inside what is clearly a Globe. Not only that, but she is doing so on a motorcycle, and as if that wasn't enough the motorcycle involved is an early Indian. This confirms that, in America at least, the Globe was evolving at the same time as the Silodrome.

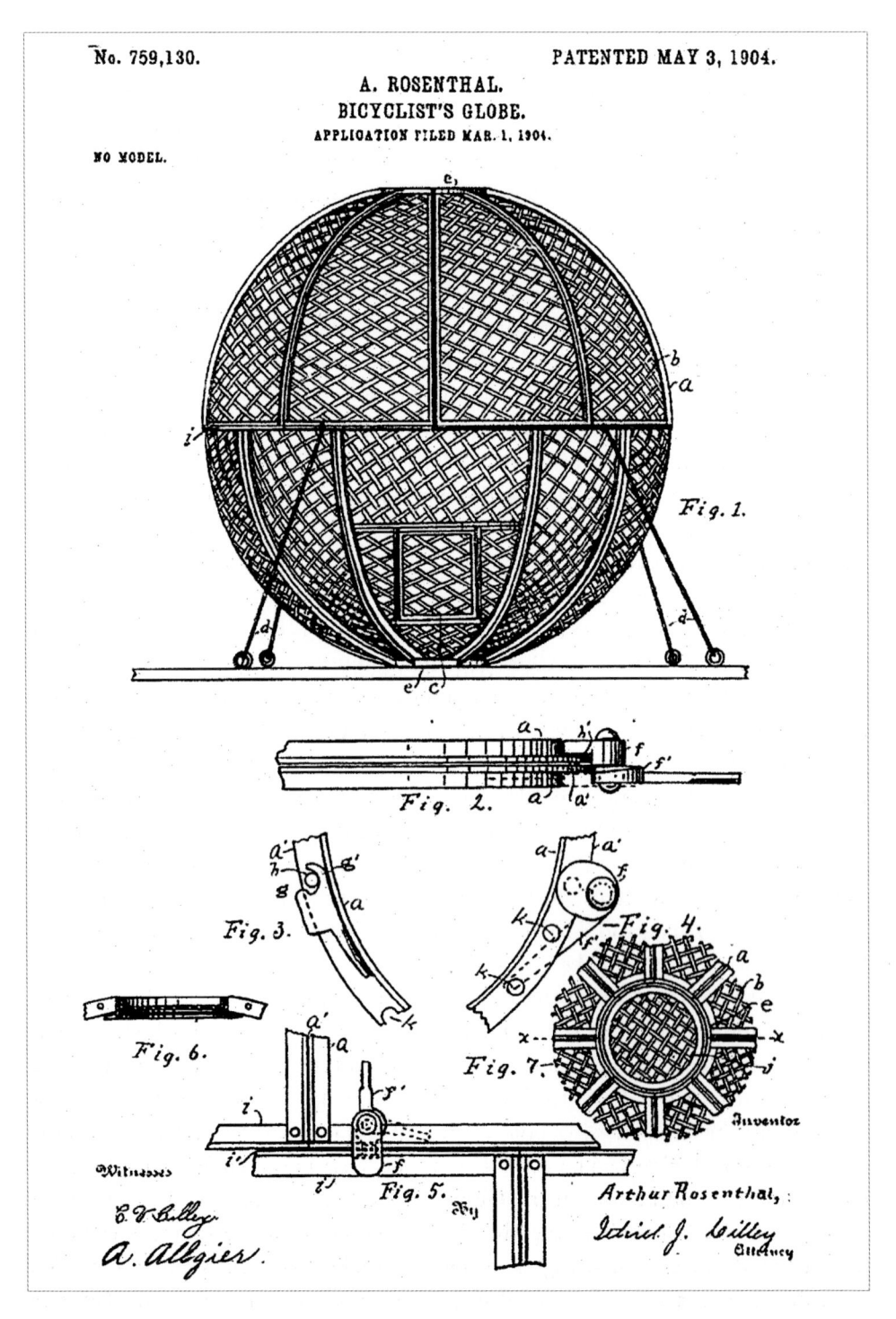

The first attempt to patent a version of the Globe, Rosenthal's Bicyclist's Globe, 1904.

THE GLOBE

Unlike the Wall, the Globe didn't seem to need a stimulus from America in order to develop in Europe, although first evidence of Globes in Europe comes a little later. The French appear to have been the leaders, with reports of Globes being manufactured in Paris in 1925 and touring mainland Europe before crossing the channel at around the same time, or possibly slightly before, the first Silodromes appeared. Credit for introducing the Globe to British audiences probably lies with John Collins, with the bikes ridden by the previously mentioned Abbins brothers, Paulitt and Henri.

The Abbins were former acrobats employed by Barnum's Circus, with one of the brothers renowned for pedalling his way around the towns they visited on his unicycle, a trick that may or may not have been the inspiration for Tornado Smith's later use of a penny-farthing. Another French rider around at this time was Henri Corbiere, who toured Britain with his daughter Elizabeth, including a number of seasons at Great Yarmouth, and Europe with a German woman Fraulein Lya Schmidt, with their act culminating in a loop-the-loop with a sidecar. A particular feature of Corbiere's act was a general invitation to the public to ride in the sidecar, an invitation many brave souls took up.

John Collins' brother Pat was also soon in on the act, with one report suggesting that he presented a Globe at William Irving's fairground in Dorking in 1927. John's Globe later fell into the hands of Wall of Death proprietor Tommy Messham and was revived briefly after the Second World War when it was described as 'the world's biggest cheese grater'. This Globe originated in Northern Ireland, ostensibly being made at the Harland and Wolff shipyard, and had been ridden by a male and female double act.

Like the Wall, Globes seemed to meet some of the public's need for new thrills and there are a number of reports of different Globes touring Britain in the 1930s. One of these was owned by Sam Naishtad, who went on to manage a number of Wall riders. This travelled through a number of back end fairs and later became known as 'John Collins' Globe of Death'.

Unlike the Wall, the Globe act did not seem to follow any kind of set pattern, although common features soon emerged. Some acts opened with bicyclists and most culminated in the ultimate stunt of a motorbike looping the inside of the Globe. For maximum effect two bikes would circle the interior, one following the equator and the other circling pole to pole. Naturally, this demanded immaculate timing and not all riders could manage it. Other variations therefore included bikes circling the top and bottom of the Globe or one bike passing over a cyclist or the almost inevitable lion. Other times the bikes would simply rotate around a seemingly unconcerned colleague standing in the centre, usually a woman. Many of the riders were the same as those riding the Wall, perhaps those seeking that extra challenge, for riding the Globe was undoubtedly harder than riding the Wall. Many acts liked

Above left: Corbiere and Schmidt, a French-German double act who looped the loop with a sidecar inside a Globe.

Above right: Speedy Babbs, world record holder on the Wall and Globe rider, outside his transport. (Courtesy Chuck Myles)

to demonstrate this by offering a prize of £5 to any member of the audience who could take a bike up, a challenge few accepted, whereas members of Wall audiences were less reticent in coming forward – even if they too ultimately found the act wasn't as easy as it may have looked.

Globes remained popular in Europe at this time, with the German Hugo Hasse presenting a Globe show in Hamburg around 1929 with his compatriot, circus director Julius Jager, known as 'Cliff Aeros', also running a show between 1930 and 1950. Globes were also spotted in Switzerland as well as France. They also featured in America with the early Silodrome endurance record holder and wing walker 'Speedy' Babbs continuing to demonstrate his reckless streak by performing in a Globe at night with fireworks attached to him. Already holder of the Wall endurance record, Babbs (one of the few riders to truly perfect the Loop the Loop), performed a total of 2,003 revolutions in a Globe, although this feat was never to earn him the same celebrity as his Wall record, perhaps demonstrating the relative interest in each.

In the meantime, just as Globes were finding a place on both the travelling circuit and static shows in Britain (Globes became a regular feature at Olympia for example), they found fresh competition in the form of Silodromes. As previous chapters have shown, these quickly found their way into the public's consciousness, growing in number and popularity at a rate that far outstripped the progress of the Globe. We can only speculate why the Globe seemed to lose out to its new rival. As early as the spring of 1930 the two were presented side by side by Pat Collins at Chester Races although, given legal disputes over the name of both attractions at that time, they were advertised there as 'The Drome of Satan' and 'The Globe of Terror'. Part of the reason might have been the relative speed and ease with which the wooden Walls could be built, against the effort required to construct a metal Globe. Early Globes, such as that later owned by Tommy Messham, were put together by shipbuilders, and these were felt to be the best, having a rigidity later Globes lacked. This was a slow process, however, and it meant that it was easier to get Walls out onto the fairground scene at a critical time. Furthermore, potential riders would have been attracted to the newer, and frankly less dangerous, Wall.

Other possible explanations have already been put forward, including the fact that it was much easier for mass audiences to take in and see a Wall show than one in a Globe. To this might be added the proprietor's perspective than it would have been possible to fit in more shows per hour on the Wall than in a Globe, with the latter act being physically more demanding and having a smaller pool of riders to draw on.

A very early Globe with a couple of sullen-looking riders.

RIDING THE WALL OF DEATH

The sheer razzmatazz and aura of glamour that the early American Silodromes would have brought with them from across the Atlantic, home of Hollywood and all things special at a time of Depression in Europe, should also not be underestimated. Combined with this, the money and energy of the double act of showman and entrepreneur of Pat Collins and Billy Butlin would also have been significant as they began to focus more on Walls.

Globes did not disappear, continuing to crop up at fairs throughout the pre-war years, often competing directly with one or more Walls; but they remained a novelty rather than mainstream act. A final reason for this may have been the real danger that came with the Globe. Billy Bellhouse's story has already been recounted, with an accident on the Globe ending his career in the mid-1930s. Whereas spills went with the territory, Wall riders tended to come back from their accidents. This wasn't always the way with Globe riders.

The file listing Globe-related disasters began to grow too thick for comfort. One horrific example involved Globe rider Ron Rolfe, who rode for an owner called Chipchase in the inter-war years. The act came to an abrupt halt just before the Second World War when Rolfe and Chipchase attempted a two-bike show that resulted in the two colliding and Chipchase breaking his back, confining him to a wheelchair for the rest of his life. Rolfe, meanwhile, had multiple broken bones and a number of stitches and was plagued with complaints related to the smash for the remainder of his days. Such occurrences were not unique. On one occasion during a live radio broadcast featuring a Globe show just before the outbreak of the Second World War another accident took place, this time fatal, with the commentator breaking into tears as he described the scene. The Globe was attracting a bad press, which would have reverberated with both the public and riders, although this never seemed to be quite enough to finish the attraction off for good.

The need to push the limits of the attraction seemed to motivate some of the more daring of riders, with a particular example being the creation of a new airborne act constructed by the father of the speedway and Wall rider Skid Skinner in 1936. Borrowing from some of the earlier Edwardian acts, this involved an aerial track ride combined with an element of trapeze, the two counterbalancing each other above the heads of the crowd with a third performer transferring his weight along a pair of track bars.

After the Second World War Globes reappeared, but there seemed less of them around than before the hostilities. They cropped up in the oddest of places, including a Christmas engagement for one on the roof of Allders department store in Croydon. A further derivation of the Globe was revealed at Bertram Mills Circus at Olympia during the 1951/52 season, but this too was to end in tragedy. Borrowing much from the old Bowl of Death bicycle rides, this was a steel mesh open torus, or doughnut

Another attempt by Speedy Babbs to provide thrills with his Cycle Whirl, a Globe variation, 1955. (Courtesy Chuck Myles)

shape, raised above the ground with riders circling the interior. The rider was Arno Wickbold, who would rev up his bike along the 'floor' of the torus and then ride up onto its walls. Once he had attained sufficient speed and force the bottom of the cage would open up, revealing him to the audience below in an echo of some of the early bicycle acts. Wickbold was a well-known stunt rider at this time and something of a showman, a fact that was to contribute to his undoing. He wore a romantic Errol Flynn flowing white shirt and one day the shirt tails got caught in the back wheel of the bike just as the cage floor opened. Within an instant the bike spluttered and began to plunge. Later reports suggested that at this point Wickbold could have saved his life by aiming for the safety net, but this would have left the bike hurtling uncontrolled towards the crowd. Valiantly, he chose to stay on the bike and direct it into the ring. The noise when he hit the floor was deafening and, after an agonising forty-eight-hour period during which he clung tenaciously onto life, he finally passed away.

Although it didn't involve an actual Globe, this accident sent shockwaves through the business and attention focused almost exclusively on the reviving Wall business. During the post-war years Globes continued to surface every now and then but, if anything, they became even more of a novelty. The Globe enjoyed a brief revival in 1977 when John Collins' original Abbins Globe came back onto the scene. This had been bought by Wall owner Tommy Messham some years before in Ireland and caught the eye of one of his riders, Allan Ford, and a friend of his, Charles Winter, a specialist in restoring Indians. Together the pair built the Globe up at the latter's farm in Surrey using available farm equipment and whatever they could lay their hands on.

There's no manual on how to ride a Globe and there was no one around to show them how, so Ford and Winter taught themselves, initially on bicycles and subsequently using two very old 1930s 98cc James motorbikes. These didn't quite have the power they needed so they traded up to some of Ford's Bantams and, using these, they were able to put an adequate show together, good enough to present to the public, Winter adopting the name 'Cliffhanger' and Ford 'Dan Dare' for the duration.

The duo started at a steam rally at Horsham one bank holiday, doing well, and then moved on to the Great Dorset Steam Fair. When they got there they found that Messham had arrived before them with his Wall and was next to their pitch. This hadn't been part of the plan as Ford was of the view by that time that a Globe couldn't compete with a Wall in terms of spectacle. The Globe was in a hired marquee and, as such, had no 'front' to pull the public in. Also, given the nature of the bikes they were using, the tent filled with fumes within minutes, limiting the length of the show.

THE GLOBE

Wickbold's Aerial Sensation, a variation of a Globe, on which Arnold Wickbold was to die.

Charles Winter's Globe, built up on a farm to allow him to learn how to ride.

The marquee used by Charles Winter and Allan Ford to present their Globe show in the late 1970s.

RIDING THE WALL OF DEATH

Messham's plans to tour the Globe and Wall together therefore didn't come to fruition and the Globe 'retired', still built up behind a pub in Godstone, before moving back to Winter's farm, where it was taken down and remains to this day. The whole experience seemed to confirm the suspicions of Ford and others that, while the Globe had a novelty appeal, it was best left as a circus act or perhaps a free attraction at something like a fête.

Perhaps one of the most interesting features of this episode is that the Globe was presented as being the first such act since the Second World War. Even allowing for a splash of showmanship, Messham must have known that this wasn't so. Globes had appeared in a number of places during that period, including J.J. Collins' 'Infernal' Globe, which had appeared at Loughborough in 1957 and Wall rider 'Speedy' Barham's Globe, which he presented at the Cattle Market in Rugby in 1962. Variations on Wickbold's Bowl of Death had also persisted through the 1950s.

The Globe also lived on in both Europe and America, with Lucky Thibeault, dubbed the 'One Man Suicide Squad', presenting a Globe in New England during the 1967-68 season, reviving a previous excursion with the Globe during 1950/51. Charles Winter also spent some time in America riding Globes. In the country with his wife, who was American, Winter had seen a Globe at a circus and stayed behind to meet the owner, Douglas MacValley. It turned out that MacValley had been busy buying up most of the Globes in America, in particular around Las Vagas, and Winter ended up touring most of the country with his Globes during 1982, including the Playboy Casino, the Ohio State Fair and the Six Flags Great Adventure in Jackson, N.J. alongside a Brazilian rider called Humberto Fonseca. Relatively late onto the Globe and Wall scene, Winter had plans to settle in America, but Messham wanted to have his Globe available for any possible European shows and MacValley operated a virtual monopoly on them in the States. At one point Winter also flew to Florida to look at a Wall for sale there, but it was so rotten that he flew back. Over the years Winter corresponded regularly with Lucky Thibeault, and it was through these letters that he discovered that Thibeault took up Silodrome riding again in 1989 after a twenty-five-year break!

Since Messham's attempted revival the Globe has proved its resilience by refusing to fade away, with the occasional enthusiasts keeping the flame alive. Two such men were Eddie Sloane, a one-time sand racer, and Niall O'Connor, who together spent eighteen months perfecting a Globe act, showing it first at the Isle of Man TT Races in 1992. Their show involved the usual range of tricks, with Sloane's girlfriend Pauline Dale standing at the base of the Globe during high-speed crossovers. The duo used a specially modified Yamaha DT125 and a Honda MTX125, both without brakes and with the suspension adjusted right down. Like many before him, Sloane commented at the time just how much harder it was to ride a Globe than the Wall,

THE GLOBE

**Performing in an 18 Foot Vertical Cage
Doing 3 Death-Defying Acts Each Show**

Act Lasts for about 15 Minutes
Space needed for cage — 30x30x10' high
Weight — Approximately 3,000 pounds

Notice — This cage requires no stakes in ground or any nailing down — can be set up on any smooth wooden stage or cement floor.

**GLOBE of DEATH and CAGE of DEATH
now both at liberty for bookings
during 1967-1968.**

**Excellent for Sport Shows, Fairs, Parks,
Circus, Shopping Centers and Celebrations.**

Right: A flyer promoting Lucky Thibeault's US Globe show. (Courtesy Charles Winter)

Below: A 100cc James motorcycle as used in the Globe show.

prophetic words as it turned out that during the show he hit a patch of anti-freeze and water, which had leaked from one of the over-heating bikes and slid to the base of the Globe, fortunately without sustaining any injury.

O'Connor cropped up again towards the end of the decade partnering Globe owner Adrian Hastings. Although it is not known if this was the same Globe, publicity accompanying the act suggested it had toured Europe, the Middle East and Hong Kong, as well as appearing at a number of top indoor UK venues such as the London Arena, Manchester's G-Mex Centre and the Sheffield Arena, as well as a stint outdoors at the Bristol hot air balloon convention in 1999. In the same year the Globe appeared on the British Saturday evening TV show *Don't Try This At Home*. This Globe is known to have continued into the early part of the new century and was last sighted giving a charity show in its home town of Preston in January 2005.

These days the most active guardians of the Globe are probably the Varanne brothers, based appropriately enough in France. Known as the Infernal Varanne, this act features three brothers: Danny, who leads the act, alongside Philippe and Gerard, who have been riding since 1984. Their father owned and operated a Wall of Death, which the brothers also run. (As an aside, the Varannes keep their hatch door open during performances, a feature also common in Germany.) The Globe is their passion though, with the act starting in 1992. Like the British Globe, the Infernal Varanne has toured the world doing a series of short, ten-minute shows, with two or three riders. The Varannes use bikes with four-stroke engines in order to minimize the smoke and fumes and to make the attraction more indoor-friendly, and tour with their own 15-foot container. Once again, the show features a woman standing at the base of the Globe. Occasionally, the Varannes offer a Globe and Wall combination, such as at the 'Circus Medrano' in Italy in 1994, and during the subsequent season through Germany and Austria, when they toured with the German wall rider Martin Bloomer.

The Globe has just about survived into the twenty-first century, which has to be a testament to its enduring attraction considering the chequered history it has endured during the hundred or so years it has been around. That it has done so can probably be put down in part to the alternative it offers to the Wall of Death – of the same family, but definitely different. More dangerous, more highly skilled perhaps, but less easy to manage and less accessible. To the cognoscenti it is the ultimate expression of gravity-defying motorbike acts, but lay audiences didn't always see it that way. History is littered with examples of cases where the technically superior out of two alternatives loses out in the race for dominance, VHS and Betamax for example, and maybe this is another one of those?

If the Globe has suffered a chequered history, what happened to the Wall after the Second World War, and in what state did it enter the new century? It is time to return to our main story.

SIX

THE SHOW GOES ON

As the Second World War began, cinema audiences were entertained by George Formby, one of the biggest stars of the day, in a film called *Spare a Copper*. In this film Formby played a war reserve policeman trying to join the motorcycle squad who prevents a plot by enemy spies to blow up a new warship. A particular feature of the film was what film critic Brendan Ryan described as a 'stomach churning' sequence on a Wall of Death. Incidentally, Formby himself was a big motorcycle fan, in particular Arials, a secret he kept from his wife.

In 1950, with war behind them, audiences returned to see a young Laurence Harvey, playing a prizefighter caught up in a spot of bother with a wall rider. Originally called 'There is Another Sun', this film was renamed *The Wall of Death* and featured some spectacular riding by Jimmy Kynaston and Jake and a young Tommy Messham, who was actually serving his national service in the RAF at the time. The Wall, it seemed, had become an everyday part of British entertainment, part of the mainstream, with war apparently doing little to shift its status.

On the outbreak of war most Walls had pulled over, the combination of mechanical expertise and sheer young daredevilry they had involved being absorbed into the greater war effort. Early Wall pioneer George Todd's experience was typical. Despite having just bought his own Wall with his wife, 'Fearless' Winnie Souter, he spent the duration in his caravan outside Weston-super-Mare where exercised his skills working for Hawker Siddley.

Staying in one place for more than a week clearly had an impact in other ways as it was here that their daughter Ann was born, although after a protracted two-day labour Winnie was advised by her doctor not to have any more children, the delay in delivery being attributed to the abnormally strong abdominal muscles she'd acquired as a result of being a Wall of Death rider. Together they sat out the Second World War, doing their bit but biding their time. As soon as peace returned George was back with his wife working their Wall at Ramsgate's Merrie England. Likewise, George's brother Frank, who'd been touring Italy when war broke out, causing him to lose his Wall, picked up where he'd left off, presenting a new Wall at Battersea. Other key figures followed suit, with Eddy Monte travelling a Wall at Pat Collins' fair (although Pat himself had died in 1943), and Elias Harris, who'd worked as an aviation fitter in Southampton during the conflict, also returning with his Wall.

Many Walls survived the war physically, and perhaps part of the reason they were able to make such a rapid return to the fairground scene was their relative solidity, which made them easy to store, along with the absence of a need to source fresh parts to get them going again – bearing in mind that many standard fairground rides had been brought in from Germany and there were more pressing demands on engineering capacity. Furthermore, Walls hadn't entirely gone to ground during the Second World War, with one or two popping up as part of the Government's plan to encourage 'Holidays at Home'.

Under this initiative local authorities were encouraged to put together a programme of amusements over the summer months in order to dissuade people from travelling on the railways, which were being increasingly pressed into service for the transfer of troops and preparations for D-Day. Walls occasionally made an appearance at these events, although finding enough experienced young riders must have made it difficult to put on more than a token show. These shows were naturally held under blackout conditions, leading to the odd sight of the bright lights surrounding the show being hidden under camouflage netting. The Second World War had another knock-on benefit for travelling Walls in that ex-War Department lorries and trailers flooded onto the market, many of which were perfect for transporting Walls. Many Octopus rides around this time were actually built on old searchlight trailers.

As happened after the First World War the price of victory soon became apparent. This time round though, there were a number of critical differences. Everyone in the country had been subject to the austerities of war and had spent a long time promising themselves something better when hostilities ceased. While the idea of Holidays At Home may have satisfied the public during the conflict itself, they were looking for a bit more in the way of entertainment after it. There was a pent-up demand for fun as people became free from the straitjacket of curfews, rationing and blackouts. Another key difference was that, although plenty of young men never came home, many more did; and they too were in the market for some fun. The sheer scale of loss of young men, while still terrible, did not match that of the previous conflict. London and a number of the country's great cities may have been in ruins, bananas may have still been in short supply and money may have been tight, but that didn't mean you couldn't go out and enjoy yourself.

THE SHOW GOES ON

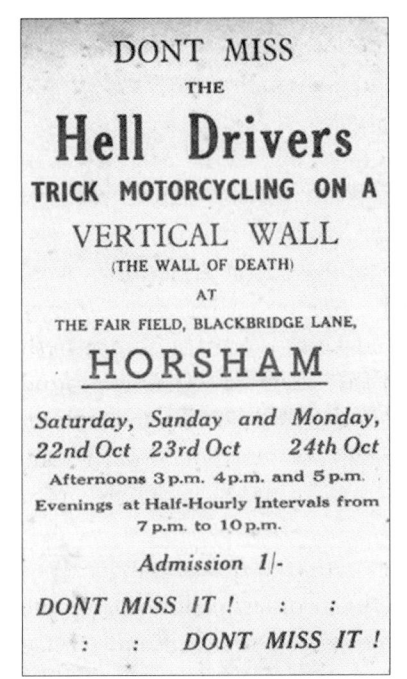

Above: Eddie Monte's Wall, Birmingham 1949, the Wall later bought by Tommy Messham. Note the three sets of stairs.

Left: Poster advertising the Hell drivers at Horsham after the Second World War.

One fly in the ointment was again the economy. Following the pattern after the previous war the outlook was bleak. Moving back onto a peace footing after having reorganised the entire economy to fight the Second World War took time. Huge stocks of absolute wealth had been used up, making it difficult to reinvest in industry. The pound was hopelessly overvalued and unconditional financial support from the US had been converted into a loan with conditions attached. Then there was the weather – the winter of 1946/47 being the harshest in memory, as if the people hadn't suffered enough.

While all this was going on the new Labour Government was embarking upon a hugely ambitious programme of social change on the basis that state control had won the war so now it could win the peace. Things were going to change. There was a lot going on, but taking all things into consideration this was a time of hope, even if it wasn't always underpinned by expectation. In another echo of the post-First World War period the Government decided to cheer everyone up with a grand gesture: The Festival of Britain. Held in 1951, this both marked the centenary of Prince Albert's original Great Exhibition while at the same time offering a celebration of the nation's science, culture and history. Events were held across the country although two more permanent sites were established on London's South Bank and at the Festival Pleasure Gardens in Battersea, and it seemed only natural that the latter included a Wall of Death: Frank Todd's Hell Riders. Despite losing his original

RIDING THE WALL OF DEATH

Wall to the Italians, Todd was back in business and a key attraction at the country's premier entertainment hotspot, where he gained a prime pitch just underneath the Big Dipper, the track of which passed by the bally outside the Wall.

As the 1950s got under way a new age began to dawn and the Wall of Death had its place in it. After the Second World War some new faces had also appeared on the scene, including the highly respected and well-liked Doug Murphy from Colne in Lancashire. Initially starting out in 1947, after a war spent as a despatch rider and toying with the idea of a career in speedway, Murphy earned an international reputation, riding in his time in locations as far flung as Hawaii, Israel and Russia, as well as most countries in Western Europe. Murphy gained a particular following in Germany, where his more flamboyant style contrasted with the more staid approach of the locals and he was to be found riding at the Oktoberfest in Munich most years.

Murphy was not unique in this popularity, British trick riders in particular often being invited to ride in Germany, where the money was good and the set up was convenient. Riders could ride at the Oktoberfest, come home and go out again for the Hamburg Domfest. Also, German walls would alternate their trick riders on the basis that members of the public would pay twice to see different riders rather than the general assumption in Britain that customers paid to see a generic show rather than specific personalities.

Murphy was a showman. One specialty, along with the usual repertoire of tricks and stunts, was to pretend to be drunk, falling flat on his face before even mounting his bike. He was also resilient, counting two broken noses, broken ribs, arms and legs along the course of his near-thirty year career. By some miracle none of these accidents occurred during his stint in Las Vagas, during which he discovered that someone had been dropping pep pills into his coffee to spice things up a bit. Murphy went on to have a long and varied career, including riding 'four on a Wall' at the Neu-Ulm Carnival in Germany in May 1957 and three years spent in Israel in the early 1960s, where he also claimed to break the world record for riding the Wall. Despite such a diverse lifestyle, Murphy still returned home to Lancashire every winter to recuperate and, although he could boast an international reputation, his earnings were not sufficient to carry him through to the spring and Murphy would often take part-time work such as pumping petrol. He was his own man though and kept his own bike, an Indian naturally, which he used to keep in the downstairs room of his modest one-up one-down back-to-back terrace house in Colne.

If it could have talked, the bike itself could have told some stories. It found its way to England with the American rider Earl Ketring in 1929, where it had appeared at the Kursaal in Southend as well as in Berlin, being sold to rider Bill Miller when Ketring returned home in 1936. Miller managed to smuggle the bike out of Russia when he was appearing in Leningrad and the authorities were on his case, something

THE SHOW GOES ON

DO NOT FAIL TO VISIT

THE WALL OF DEATH

(Promenade, Gravesend Regatta Week, August 15th, 1949.)
Introducing The World's No. 1 Riders

The Internationally Famous Death Dodgers

In a Show that Thrills and Amazes

Boston Bob
International Champion in His Original Trick & Stunt Act

Speedy Dug Murphy
The Flying Irishman. Acknowledged World's Fastest Wall Rider

Cyclone Jake
One of the original Hell's Angels and without a doubt One of The Most Experienced Riders of To-day.

A SHOW FOR YOUNG AND OLD THAT NEVER FAILS TO PLEASE.

HERE FOR ONE WEEK ONLY.

Above left: A poster calling people to Jake Messham's show, riding alongside Dug [sic] Murphy and Boston Bob in 1949. (Courtesy Ken Fox)

Above right: A signed photo of Roy Swift – international stunt rider – taken at Elstree Studios 1949.

that seems to be a feature of foreign riders' involvement in that country. The bike then passed to Peter Catchpole who eventually sold it to Murphy, although not before it had been to Australia, Nigeria and Liberia with him. With Murphy it travelled to America, Hawaii, Mexico and Japan. Murphy rode with Jimmy Kynaston in Germany, another rising star of the Wall whose story is covered in greater detail later on. Other leading riders at this time included Roy Swift and Harry Holland, who were riding as a double act at Belle Vue in Manchester by 1948. Holland had been operating before the Second World War and took Swift on the previous year after Swift had approached him and impressed with his experience of jumping bikes over cars.

Swift learned over the following winter, practising in the mornings and preparing the bikes for the following Easter's opening in the afternoon. On one occasion Swift was breaking in some new tyres, going round the Wall to get the right slope on them. A mesmeric job, during which it was easy to lose your sense of speed, Swift was helped by Holland banging once on the centre pole if he thought he was going

Jimmy Kynaston and Jake Messham and an unknown rider wearing a skull and crossbones Wall of Death top.

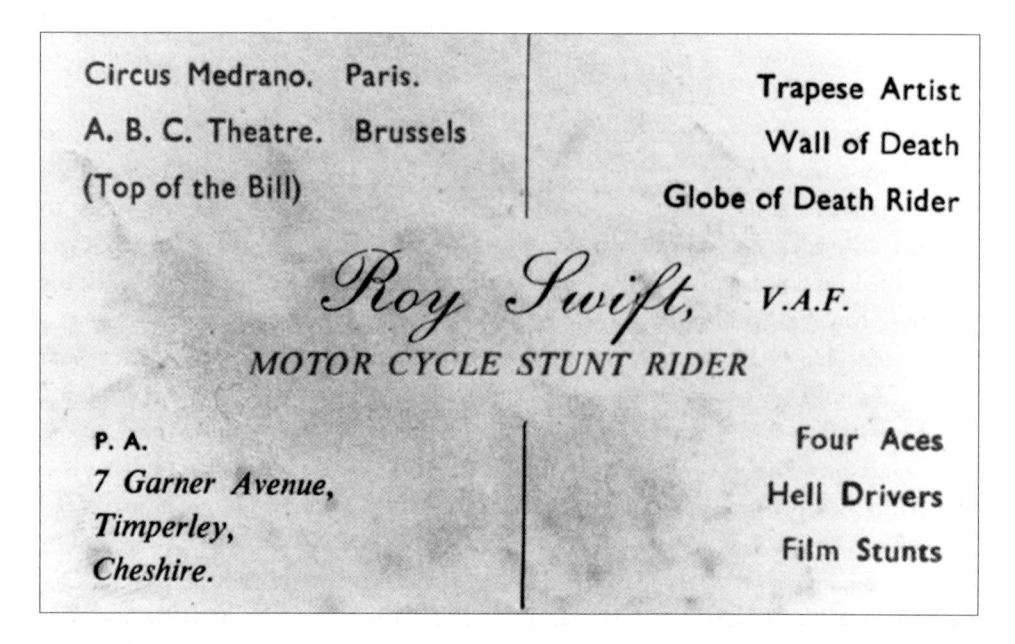

Circus Medrano. Paris.	Trapese Artist
A. B. C. Theatre. Brussels	Wall of Death
(Top of the Bill)	Globe of Death Rider

Roy Swift, V.A.F.
MOTOR CYCLE STUNT RIDER

P. A.	Four Aces
7 Garner Avenue,	Hell Drivers
Timperley,	Film Stunts
Cheshire.	

Roy Swift's business card, describing a range of roles from trapeze artist to Globe of Death rider.

Harry Holland, Jean Holland and Roy Swift at Belle Vue, Manchester just after the Second World War.

too slow and twice if he was going too fast. Despite this, Swift felt his rear tyre go and he fell, breaking a leg. A smiling Holland picked him up, and when challenged as to why he left him to fall, Holland replied that he was curious to see how slow an Indian could go before it fell.

Somehow their friendship remained intact and they stayed together for the best part of ten years with Swift performing both the dips and dives of death and the Race of Death and Holland most of the trick riding. Holland was one of the few riders to master riding backwards with no hands. Swift left in the late 1950s as demand for the Wall trailed off and he was offered other things, leaving to become a trapeze artist for the Australian Air Aces, which started a career in the circus, including some time as a Globe rider. Harry Holland went on to tour the continent, at one point being kept in Russia until he'd taught two of their people to ride. He also had a bit of bad luck in Sweden when he was mauled on the Wall by a lioness that grabbed him by the neck. His partner Swift described his body as 'like a battlefield' after this. Holland had two partners, operating another permanent Wall at New Brighton and a third that they toured in the South, and included his wife Jean in the act. One of these Walls was slightly smaller to take a car. After leaving the Wall he went on to manage an amusement park in New Zealand, and it is Holland's bike that the modern-day rider Ken Fox still rides today.

RIDING THE WALL OF DEATH

Swift was one of a new breed of riders now emerging onto the scene. They differed from the pre-war generation, the pioneers, in that many of them were taught the basic techniques of how to ride the Wall, whereas most of their predecessors had had to teach themselves – other riders being potential competitors for business and therefore reluctant to train someone who might become a possible rival for a job. While basic technique could be taught, as with all true entertainers there was no substitute for flair and talent.

Billy Butlin, who remained a major Wall operator for some years after the Second World War, perhaps recognised more than most the divide between having basic skills and being a good trick rider. While he continued to rent his walls out he also had his own permanent Wall set up at Skegness that he used to train up riders to straight ride, supplementing these with specialist trick riders who he'd supply with one of his walls. One of the new breed of riders around this time, Roy Cripsey, whose family had had Walls during the glory days, started off as a combination of trainer and trick rider. This new generation soon showed the same streak of individuality that characterised their predecessors, and Wall owners would often be left in the lurch by a rider who promised one thing and delivered another. One classic example of this occurred in 1949 when Albert Evans had a run of fairs covering Scotland and had booked Jake Messham to ride for him. Part way through the run Messham simply disappeared, saying he had something he had to attend to. Although he didn't say so at the time, that 'something' was trick riding for the filming of *The Wall of Death*, which came out the following year. In the meantime, Evans was forced to engage a fresh rider, Frank Todd, and at first the partnership was a successful one, with Todd proving his dexterity by taking an Austin Seven up on the Wall. Having parked his Wall up, Todd then failed to turn up himself for the following season, the better offer in his case being his spot at the Festival of Britain. An exasperated Evans eventually sued for the loss of rents and after a couple of years won £900 damages, although the sum was swallowed by legal costs.

Similar tales were commonplace, from riders disappearing because of woman trouble to someone not being available because he'd gone home to 'sign on' for unemployment benefit. Other times the police might be involved, in which case the rider might expect some protection from his fairground 'family', who would close ranks to protect one of their own. Perhaps this experience was the final straw for Evans, who decided to get out of the Wall business shortly afterwards, going so far as to break up his Wall. After a break of around four years he was back though, buying an American-made Wall off Tommy Wrighton in Southport, which the family continued to tour until 1968. It was not as if any great shift had taken place in demand for the Wall; Evans' decision seems to have been motivated more by the heart than the head. Like so many others, Evans had found that the Wall can permeate your system, becoming a way of life. The team required to run it become

THE SHOW GOES ON

The front of Albert Evans' Wall with father, daughter Norma and son Albert jnr – the father spieling and the son waiting to ride. (Courtesy Albert Evans)

part of your family. When everyone has to rely on everyone else to do their job bonds of trust build up that become hard to break and, even long after they've stopped riding, Wall riders need little encouragement to reminisce about their times on the Wall and the experiences they had.

At least a dozen Walls have been formally recorded in Britain from this time, although it is likely that there were many more than this, if not quite the number there were operating during the pre-war glory days. This compares with a figure of seventeen recorded in the US[24]. As well as those already mentioned these included Ron Miller's Wall at New Brighton, Jake Messham's at Hampstead Heath and Freddy Heywood's at Cleethorpes. Another Wall belonged to Len Parker, the unfortunate rider who died when his Wall fell on him during a pull down, who'd actually bought a Wall during the Second World War to use at 'Holiday at Home' events. He was partnered at first by Johnny Parr, but he was to break his leg at Lincoln, causing Len to call upon his brother Horace, who'd been riding on various walls since 1934. Despite the possible repercussions, Horace answered the call and took the serious step of fleeing his wartime job. The two brothers became partners and travelled under the banner of Marshall's Modern Amusements for many years until both they and the Wall were worn out, a factor that may have contributed to Len's ultimately fatal accident. Horace went on to ride for Roy Cripsey, whose brother Graham also travelled a Wall during the late 1940s.

The continued success of the Wall of Death around this time can perhaps be attributed in part to a more general rising interest in motorbikes, which were the chosen and most affordable mode of transport for a large proportion of the working population. On finishing their apprenticeship a young man would typically go out and buy a motorbike and when he got married and kids came along he'd be more likely to add a sidecar on to carry them around than take the expensive step of buying a car.

During the 1950s the number of licensed motorbikes on British roads more than doubled to around one-and-a-half million. Another reflection of this growth in interest was the rise of speedway as a sport, which drew crowds comparable to modern football gates at their stadiums. Considerable cross-over existed between speedway and Wall riders, although each tended to have their own advocates and prejudices. Ronnie Moore, two-time world speedway champion in 1954 and 1959, is perhaps the most notable example of someone who switched between the two, going on to tour on a Wall in his native New Zealand in the 1950s and 1960s, and Roy Swift also raced at Belle Vue, Bradford and Halifax speedways.

Riding, be it on the Wall or round a track, had retained its status as a gateway to stardom and riches and plenty of young men were prepared to risk their neck to achieve these prizes. Not just men either. The by-now well-established tradition of women riders continued after the Second World War including the likes of Maureen Swift, Winnie Souter and Betty Ellis, although Alma Skinner stopped riding.

Maureen Kelly lived at her parents' bed and breakfast in Southend and it was inevitable that at some point she'd see the Wall at the Kursaal. In 1947 she promptly fell in love with what she saw, along with Tornado's brand of showmanship that went with it. Although still only fifteen, Maureen had left school the year before and had already been through a succession of jobs. When she saw Tornado's Wall she knew what she wanted to do. After five weeks of evening practice she was able to go up on the Wall and the following year was performing in up to thirty shows a day, a combination of straight riding, snake trails and side-saddle. Before long her fame spread. Maureen changed her name to Swift and, by 1950, she was performing at New Brighton with riders Jack Campbell and Ricky Dare and two years later was performing as a guest at Bertram Mills' Circus at Olympia. In the meantime, however, she'd heard that a Wall had become available and her parents bought it for her as an eighteenth birthday present. The whole family subsequently got involved, with her mother sewing the costumes and her father working the cash box. 1952 turned out to be a seminal year, as Maureen's Wall was badly damaged in a fire and she was offered work with Arno Wickbold on the Strato-Globe, an offer she fortunately

THE SHOW GOES ON

Cliff and Betty Ellis on Kitty Muller's Wall in Germany. (Courtesy Betty Ellis)

declined as this was shortly before Wickbold's fatal accident on that attraction. Instead, Maureen went to Germany where she rode on Herbert Wissinger's Wall and married a fellow rider called Siegfried Sluppke. Swift abandoned the Wall shortly after the birth of her daughter in 1958 and died in 1975 aged only forty-three.

Winnie Souter had revived her riding days at Merrie England in Ramsgate just after the Second World War and went on to ride in Zurich in 1949 and then at the Oktoberfest three years later where, after 303 shows in seventeen days, she ended her Wall-riding days on a high.

Betty Ellis was born Ullia Wissinger in Split to a Croatian mother and German father. From the start she had performing blood in her veins as both her parents worked in the circus. The horses there gave Ullia asthma, however, and she grew up with her grandmother. Determined to follow a life similar to her parents she was attracted to the fairgrounds, where she fell in love with the Wall of Death at the age of sixteen. In a newspaper interview[25] given in the 1990s Ellis described how she was taken under the wing of the German rider Kitty Muller and took to the Wall immediately. After just a year, however, she was rounded up with other fairground folk at the Oktoberfest in Munich and sent to Dachau concentration camp where she spent the rest of the Second World War, fairground folk being alien to Nazi perceptions of the master race. She survived though and came to England as she'd heard there were plenty of Walls there. She started riding on a Wall owned by Bill Miller in 1948 at New Brighton under the name of 'Miss Betty', before going on to the Kursaal at Southend where she met and married Cliff Ellis. The pair then returned to New Brighton when the Wall there was bought by Peter Catchpole. Over the following years they rode with all the main names in the Wall business including Jake Messham, Eddie Monte, Albert Evans and the Todds as well as sixteen years in Germany, riding for Pinders in Barcleona and in Italy during the winter. They last rode in the 1970s with Gustav Kokos and Yvonne Stagg at Dreamland in Margate, with Betty taking the hint that age and other physical changes were catching up with her when she found audiences laughing at her for keeping one hand on her chest in order to contain her inordinately large breasts as she circled the Wall! After Cliff's death while fishing in 1996 Betty met up again with Wall rider Ginger Joe Regan and the pair got married.

Women riders remained a feature of the Wall at the Kursaal, Southend, which was still run by the pre-war King of the Wall, Tornado Smith. Still the showman, Smith had clearly used the Second World War to ponder the future of the Wall and, it seems, come to the conclusion that it might not have one; or that if it did he'd run out of ideas of ways in which he could continue to stand out from the crowd.

His response was to plan a new attraction, the 'Loop of Death', which resembled a Wall placed on its side with a 'mouth' 15 feet in diameter and a depth of 25 feet with a tapered bowl-shaped end, looking much like a ship's ventilator. The basic idea was similar to the Wall, with riders – Tornado anticipated more than one – 'looping the loop' inside the large wooden cylinder. Rather than being 'stuck' to the side, riders would circle overhead using 125cc Royal Enfield Flying Fleas[26]. The whole thing had been made by Smith himself using his practiced carpentry skills, the project taking two years to complete.

It is possible that Smith was prescient in foreseeing the eventual tail-off in demand for the Wall, although the suspicion must remain that he was looking for some way of maintaining his own personal pre-eminence, which by that time was beginning to fade. He also appreciated the deficiencies of the Globe in terms of audience access, something he hoped his new Loop would address, although it is difficult to see how.

The Loop turned out to be extremely difficult to master, with only rider, Peter Catchpole, ever truly conquering it. Whether it was this or another reason, the Loop failed to grab the public's attention and before too long Smith was back entertaining audiences exclusively on his Wall. Of course, Smith was already well known for involving women on his Wall, and he adopted this feature as his gimmick, training up a rider called Julie French who was to go on to ride with him for a number of years, resurrecting the 'Gymkhana Girl' trick last performed with his wife before the Second World War.

One feature he did not revive was the use of a lion. Sadly all British Wall owners had had to put their lions down during the Second World War when there simply wasn't the meat to feed them. They had left their legacy though, and many of the Walls from around this time still had rings inside the banking where lions had once been tethered. Also, as time went on, some Walls had to be shortened as the urine from the lions had rotted the base of the panels. Lions continued to pull the crowds in America during the 1950s, where they had been less of a problem. Perhaps the greatest exponents of so-called 'Liondromes' across the Atlantic were the Pelaquin family, who used to breed their own beasts, it being illegal to import them. Their most famous lion was called King, who came to a sad end when he had to be put down after biting the arm of a drunken worker who'd reached into the lion's cage in order to impress some women friends.

Walls also maintained their popularity elsewhere after the Second World War, including in Australia, where there was a Wall ridden by one Norby Batchelor[26]. This was almost certainly the 'Hell Riders' Wall owned and ridden by Herb and Frank Durkin and their sister, known as the Dare Devil Durkins, who had toured the Australian Agricultural circuit with their Wall. The Durkins also built their own Globe which they used to supplement the Wall.

We have already seen how in Europe the German rider Pitt Löffelhardt had kept his hand in during the hostilities, and he was soon on the road again, appearing for the occupying American troops in 1946 and at the replacement for the Oktoberfest the same year. Pitt continued to ride with Kitty Muller until 1949 when he decided to give up the Wall in favour of a travelling ice business. Sadly, he was killed the following year in a car accident although his name lives on with 'Pitt's' an almost generic term for the Wall in his home country.

Another German Wall legend, Heinz Meiners, had spent the war as a courier, for part of the time at the Russian front. Meiners rode a number of walls, including that of his compatriots Herbert and Irene Wissinger, and continued to do so through the 1950s and 1960s, wearing his characteristic black britches, white shirt and black pullover, riding with Kitty Muller at the end of the 1960s when the Wissingers stopped operating their Wall. Meiners ended up riding for fifty-one years, during which time he crashed around two-dozen times – less than one every other year, not such a bad average.

Back in Britain Walls continued to do good business through the 1950s, sometimes packing in four or five shows an hour where there was a good pool of day trippers or perhaps on a Bank Holiday, a pace the riders would sustain for up to ten hours.

RIDING THE WALL OF DEATH

A Leyland lorry fully laden with a Wall, waiting to pull off a ground, 1950s. (Messham Archive)

Outside the spieler would be said to be 'walking on eggs', playing to a large crowd, using his expertise to 'turn the tip' or create the momentum within the crowd that saw them move as one towards the box office and up the steps to the walkround. The main constraint on getting customers through at this pace was the speed with which they could be got up and down the stairs. Although lucrative, this pace represented both a compromise on the sort of show presented, a cut down, no-frills, high-thrills show, and was crippling to the riders. What was more, during this period conditions for riders had shown little improvement since Garlicky Bill the Tayleur's day, with fried food, poor digs and life a continual battle against dirt still the norm. Whether they lived in digs or had their own kip trucks riders were dependent on local 'slipper' baths run by local authorities, a feature that was disappearing off the social map as more and more houses gained their own bathrooms.

No big amusement park or holiday camp was complete without a Wall during this time, but a series of subtle shifts were beginning to take place that were ultimately to have a significant impact upon the attraction. Notwithstanding the popularity of mods and rockers, motorbike ownership peaked in 1960 and, although the decline was gradual at first, the availability of affordable cars signalled a rapid fall in the numbers on the road during the decade from 1965. At the same time traditional fairs suffered from changing public tastes, which seemed to demand something more sophisticated than the traditional fairground. This was partly a perception – those that visited still enjoyed themselves – but fairs seemed to belong increasingly to another era. Many of the traditional gaffs, some of them centuries old, began to be concreted over to become car parks or shopping centres. The number of travelling fairs also declined, with quite a few going bankrupt. Later on, amusement parks offered similar thrills to the traditional fair, but in a more antiseptic and 'family-friendly' environment.

The public had alternative entertainments they could turn to. Independent television shook up the starched shirt approach of the BBC in 1955 and with the advent of cheap charter flights abroad the idea of holidaying at a Butlins Holiday Camp suddenly seemed more than a little passé. As large towns became less dependent upon single industries the tradition of wakes weeks and communal holidays also became a thing of the past. At the same time, the labour intensity of the Wall was working against it. The need to employ gaff lads for both build-up and pull-down meant they were less profitable than other rides, especially those that simply folded down from their trailers. They also increasingly stood out from the crowd, being an entertainment rather than an electrical, instant thrill ride and were beginning to look a bit dated.

Taken together, this series of blows began to make an impact on the Wall of Death. Even the great Tornado Smith decided to call it a day in 1965, selling his Wall to one of the women then riding for him, Yvonne Stagg, whose story is explored in greater detail later in this book. Smith disappeared to Spain and from there went on to live in a caravan in South Africa, where he died in 1971 by falling from a hospital window. As perhaps befits the man, even Smith's death was surrounded in publicity as it turned out that, although he was to leave a considerable estate, he was sued for bankruptcy for monies owed to both the Inland Revenue and his solicitor shortly before he died. As an aside, Smith would have just lived to read stories of his former wife Doris, by then a bus conductress, who hit the national headlines in February 1970 when, with a certain irony, she failed to pass her moped test after sixteen attempts.

Shortly before he exited the stage, Smith also left another legacy in the form of a rider called Peter Catchpole, whom he taught to ride the Wall. Catchpole was to become one of the most exotic personalities involved with the Wall during its declining years, and his too is a story recounted in more detail in the following chapter.

During the late 1960s and early 1970s Walls became a rarer sight. In 1968 Albert Evans sold his Wall to Tommy Messham, their contretemps from nearly twenty years before apparently forgiven when Jake had left Albert's father in the lurch in favour of the glamour of Ealing Studios. This represented the second time the Evans family had decided to retire the Wall business, although the bug never quite left their system

A signed photo of Harry Holland to Yvonne Stagg, wishing her 'Best wishes and good luck'.

Albert Evans' Wall of Death bus with his Wall in the background. (Courtesy Albert Evans)

and they continued to dabble with Walls in the following years. In a sign of the way things were moving one of these had to be smuggled out of the fence of the Butlins at Filey south of Scarborough when it closed down in order to save it from the liquidators.

By the late 1960s Evans had taken on his father's nickname of 'Cyclone Al', but he was getting married and had come to the conclusion that although it had been fine for his own father to encourage him to become a rider he didn't see there being enough of a future in it for any son of his. Besides, Evans had already had three bad spills and was sensible enough to appreciate that the 'big one' was only ever a matter of time away. Either the Wall or the bike would get you in the end and life as a rider was too energy-sapping to allow him to pursue other interests.

Buying a Wall was Messham's only way of staying in the business, as his father Jake refused to sell his Wall, which he continued to tour, for a while in competition with his son. While this may have been because he shared Albert Evans's views on the Wall's long-term future it's equally likely that he simply didn't want to part with it. Although there were discussions in 1970 between Jake and Albert Evans, with the latter contemplating a return to the Wall business, nothing became of it and Jake's Wall ended up rotting away in his yard.

With the Wall came a number of fairground grounds or places and these gave Messham an itinerary with which to build a business. Evans' Wall was in fact Messham's second and he bought it mainly for these places, which included many of the big fairs such as Kirkcaldy, Hull, Newcastle Town Moor, Nottingham Goose Fair, Bridgewater, Hull, Cambridge Midsummer Fair, Southampton Common at Easter, St Giles Oxford and the Bonfire Fairs around Birmingham. For most people of a certain age today who have seen a Wall in action during their childhood it would have been Messham's show they saw. It wasn't long before Messham's was the last remaining travelling Wall in the country, so rapid was the decline in the attraction. In his time Messham was to employ most of the remaining riders such as Cliff and Betty Ellis, Gerry de Roy and Doug Murphy, as well as training up some new talent, notably Freddie White, who rode as Freddie Lee and later became a milkman, Chris Lee (no relation), these days possibly the best rider still plying his trade, and Allan Ford, who was later to play an important part in keeping the Wall alive after Messham.

Gerry de Roy's career echoed the fortunes of the Wall around this time, and shows how the circle of owners and riders became ever tighter and closer, with paths crossing with the regularity of riders performing the Race of Death. Starting in 1956 with Eddie Monte, de Roy (real name Gerry Jones) then rode for Albert Evans before moving on to Roy Cripsey's Wall in Aberavon. In between these stints he rode in Germany and twice went to ride in Dubai with Peter Catchpole before ending his career with Allan Ford.

Albert Evans jnr tinkering with a bike between shows. (Courtesy Albert Evans)

There was still some demand for the Wall as the 1960s became the 1970s. In 1972 Gerry and Doug Murphy found themselves running Albert Evans' old Wall for Tommy Messham for a season at Blackpool, along with Chris O'Sullivan with Tommy's father Jake, by now retired, in the cash box. O'Sullivan was to end his days after being thrown out of a window in mysterious circumstances at Norwich Christmas Fair. Joy, Tommy Messham's wife, also rode the Wall. During the Blackpool season business was so brisk that Murphy rode out two back tyres and de Roy went on to run this same Wall at Southsea.

With no new Walls being built the Wall as an attraction seemed to enter a spiral of decline, with the few examples that were left changing hands and the owners drawing upon an ever-shrinking pool of riders. Elias Harris had sold his Wall to Roy Cripsey, who rode it with his sons, although Cripsey found time to train up a new rider, Ken Fox, who later rode for many Wall proprietors and will perform an important role later on in this story. Other Walls met a less glorious end, being put to a number of different uses. One ended up housing a mini-amusement arcade

THE SHOW GOES ON

while another, Francis Manders' Wall, was adapted so it could be converted into a bingo hall in the Winter. Albert Evans broke one up to use the wood to construct a petrol go-kart track.

It was a similar story in America. By the late 1970s there was only one motordrome still operating in the New England area, traditionally the area most closely associated with the attraction, probably due to its proximity to the home of the Indian in Massachusetts. This was out on the road in 1984, but there seems to have been a gap for the six years previous to this. Unlike in Britain, where Wall owners and riders were part of a fairly close-knit community, over the years American drome riders appear to have come and gone with greater frequency, and be less likely to stick together and share information. Partly as a result of this many American Dromes ended up rotting away during this period.

While Messham's may have been the last travelling Wall in Britain, there were a handful of others that were static, including his own second Wall, Roy Cripsey's at Bottom's Amusement Park in Skegness and one in Barry Island still operating under the Pat Collins name and once run by Frank Todd. Messham's second Wall was at Southsea, but was operating as a shoestring operation. Gerry de Roy was one of the main riders there and, although occasionally helped out by others such as Allan Ford and Charles Winter, for most of the time de Roy was on his own. This proved to be a

Cripsey's Wall of Death during the 1960s.

problem on one occasion when he fell and broke his arm. The spieler outside had to borrow a rope, climb down the inside of the Wall and open the door. Before he did so de Roy is said to have announced to the crowd, 'And that, ladies and gentlemen, concludes the show for tonight,' before promptly passing out.

Tornado Smith's Southend-based Wall, which he'd sold to Yvonne Stagg, moved to Margate with the closure of the Kursaal in 1974, where she was joined by Allan Ford. Stagg also rode with her partner Gustav Kokos, although this relationship was to end in tragedy when Gustav was to die in 1976 at the hands of her lover Terry Biebuyck. Stagg never really recovered from the shock and the publicity that followed, and when she was approached by fellow Tornado-trained rider Peter Catchpole with an offer to buy her Wall and invest in it as a prelude to touring Australia she accepted. It was never to be, however, with Stagg committing suicide over the New Year of 1976/77.

Around the same time Tommy Messham's attentions had moved on to running a set of four abreast Gallopers and the amusements at Chessington Zoo, and both of his Walls were put into storage at Haymills in Birmingham. Roy Cripsey had also ended his involvement with the Wall. The few remaining riders either took up other jobs or plied their trade abroad, with Allan Ford riding in Iran for a while and Peter Catchpole taking Ken Fox with him to Australia. Doug Murphy was also still riding, but in Germany, boasting at one stage that he could earn £3,000 for a six-month season. After a spell during which it had clung to survival everything happened at once and, as the 1970s finally drew to a close to be replaced by a new decade, the Wall finally spluttered into apparent extinction in the UK.

SEVEN

IN THE BLOOD

The story of the Wall of Death is one brought alive by the characters and personalities that promoted, ran and, most importantly, rode the Wall, many of whom are listed in the 'Wall of Fame' section at the end of this book. By its very nature, the Wall acted as a magnet for those who wanted something more out of existence, to test the limits of what life could offer in full understanding of the fact that in doing so they may go too far.

These were not people, both men and women, prepared to settle for whatever society decreed as 'normal' at the time. They made their living out of the fact that they did what everyone else couldn't conceive of doing – risking everything, every day not because they had to but simply to provide entertainment. Speak to any Wall rider and they'll tell you of the adrenalin rush going round a Wall never fails to provide. They'll tell you how they enter their own 'zone', with the outside world an indecipherable blur whizzing past them. At that point they are at the centre of the universe and everyone else is a mere spectator. Some riders learn to ride, stay for a while and disappear. They seem content to have experienced that thrill and proved something to themselves. For others, however, it enters the blood. For them it's a case of 'once a Wall rider always a Wall rider', with age, rationality and practicality secondary considerations to continued pursuit of riding that Wall. Call it an obsession if you like, but once it's in your blood you're infected for life.

The Wall can enter the blood in two ways. You either get bitten by the bug or you are born with it. In Britain and the rest of Europe, although less so in America, there's been a strong tradition of 'Wall Families'. Many of these have already cropped up in telling this story, the Collins family, the Todd brothers and their wives and the Evans family being notable examples. In time, though, the involvement of these families has literally died out, with the great Jack Todd passing on in 1989.

RIDING THE WALL OF DEATH

'Cyclone' Albert Evans along with his wife Emily and Albert Sedgewick. (Courtesy Albert Evans)

IN THE BLOOD

A young Albert Evans junior riding hands-free. (Courtesy Albert Evans)

A fourth family, the Messhams, have also been mentioned and, as we shall see, they have shown perhaps the greatest longevity, their involvement with the Wall spanning the generations since it first began in the late 1920s to the present day. The Messhams, like the Evans family, were part of the showmen's elite, the Guild, and it is worth pausing a while to consider the importance of this body in protecting and maintaining the fairground scene.

Established in 1889 as a sort of trade union or voice for showmen in the face of the growing power of local government, the Guild established a number of practices designed to help protect the livelihood and interests of showmen. Over time this helped to cement traditions already strong within that community of looking out for each other's interests and forming a kind of protective 'shell' around them. This was understandable but by no means unique, being very similar to the creeds prevalent among travellers and circus folk. The strongest bond was that of family, and Guild families became the aristocracy of the fairgrounds. This covered not just immediate family but the extended family, and ceremonial occasions involving Guild members such as weddings and funerals remain very large affairs to this day. Like any family, other than being born into it, the only way in is through marriage, and for a number of generations marrying outside the Guild was frowned upon.

RIDING THE WALL OF DEATH

The Guild's power is derived in part from the understanding that if a Guild member occupies a piece of ground at a fair three years in a row they earn the right to control that pitch. Even if they don't attend themselves another year they can sub-let it to another act – providing the Guild approves of course. This system helps to explain some of the early dominance of people such as the Collins family and a little later the Evans', both of whom were Guild members. This practice led to phrases such as 'stand your ground', meaning to keep your pitch, and 'pole position' entering the common vernacular. The latter refers to the practice of the first showman arriving at a ground throwing his poles down at the best spot in order to secure it for himself. Pitches were maintained by the simple expedient of passing them to family members and weddings would often involve giving a ride to the happy couple to start them on their way, which explains the story about Pat Collins giving a Wall to his son-in-law Elias Harris as a wedding present. Equally, pitches at important fairs such as the Nottingham Goose Fair could be traded for thousands of pounds, often acting as a form of pension plan for Guild members. The Guild also acted as a self-regulatory mechanism. Tasks such as supplies or maintenance would remain within 'the family', with failure to deliver good work to a fellow member the equivalent of both professional and social suicide.

The Guild system goes some way to explaining the number of 'Wall dynasties' within Britain, and the Messham family is a good example of this. Their involvement with the Wall started with Jake Messham in the 1930s, who also worked with Pat Collins in establishing the Wall as a mainstream attraction, and the contribution made by this family to the Wall's history is perhaps not always given the recognition it deserves. Jake travelled with what became known later as 'The Big Wall' alongside his brother Edward and married into another Guild family, the Dobsons. Jake's son Tommy has already featured in this story, but he had to make his own way. He learned to ride on The Big Wall but his father refused to sell it to him for reasons unknown, although the suspicion remains that he had never quite let go of the idea of travelling with it again, despite the fact that he'd been riding for over thirty years. For a while Tommy considered not taking up the Wall as a career, working for Champion spark plugs after doing his national service as an engineer in the RAF, but he had been bitten by the bug and the Wall was in his blood. He returned to ride, including in the film *The Wall of Death* and eventually acquired his own Wall off fellow Guild member Eddie Monte in 1968.

In the course of his career Tommy became something of a legend among the Wall community, eventually having the last remaining travelling Wall. It is said by many riders that you can always spot a rider trained by Tommy Messham – they don't simply ride the Wall but give a show at the same time. Tommy was a true showman, but not always an easy man to get on with and he didn't suffer fools gladly. He was

IN THE BLOOD

A young Tommy Messham. (Messham Archive)

RIDING THE WALL OF DEATH

Tommy Messham, the maestro, riding backwards and demonstrating his showmanship. (Messham Archive)

also a good businessman and was straight with his riders, who always got paid what they were due and on time. This may have acted as some compensation for the way he sometimes treated them. There was always a very clear demarcation between boss and rider with Tommy, with riders expected to conduct menial chores such as fetching his water or emptying his chemical toilet. He could also display a temper on occasion, with screwdrivers acting as missiles an implement of choice. Tommy also earned respect not only through his riding skills (in the eyes of many Tommy was the best they ever saw) but also with his engineering skills – he could turn his hand to anything mechanical.

Tommy Messham was lucky to hit the heyday of the post-war years and, through his connections and some careful negotiating, managed to secure the best pitches across the country. It was his urgent desire to maximise throughput that could raise the stress levels and lead to occasional confrontations with riders. He married his wife Joy, unusually not a member of a Guild family, which some have speculated may have helped to account for why his father was reluctant to sell him his Wall, and they had

IN THE BLOOD

two children, Tommy junior and Julie. Tommy junior became the third generation of Messhams on the Wall and was a favourite of Jake, who gave him the Indian he used to ride as an eighteenth birthday present. Tommy junior had himself started early on the Wall, going up on the handlebars of his Dad's bike when he was as young as seven and riding on his own from age eleven, while his sister did the cash box. His father eventually gave up the Wall when he became more involved in his amusements at Chessington Zoo and Tommy junior kept going until the early 1980s although, as we shall see, the Wall was by then in his blood too and he made an attempted comeback a decade later. Perhaps by then the Wall had entered the family's DNA, as a decade after that another Messham, James, had found his own Wall and was planning to take it out on the road having trained up his sons Jake and Nathan.

In 1971 Tommy Messham senior was approached by Allan Ford. Ford had been down to Epsom Downs during Derby week and was bitten instantly by the bug. He asked Tommy if he could have a go and was told he could – so long as he used his own bike. He borrowed a Motoguzzi off his employer Don Barratt Motorcycles of Redhill and returned. For Tommy the fact that a local lad was willing to have a go was a way of pulling in more punters and he had little to lose. Although, in common with most riders, Allan failed to get up on the Wall at first he did enough to impress and he went back every night the fair was at Epsom and followed it to its next ground.

Allan Ford learning to ride on a BSA Bantam on Tommy Messham's Wall at Epsom Downs.

With the Compliments of Tommy Messham

see the WALL OF DEATH

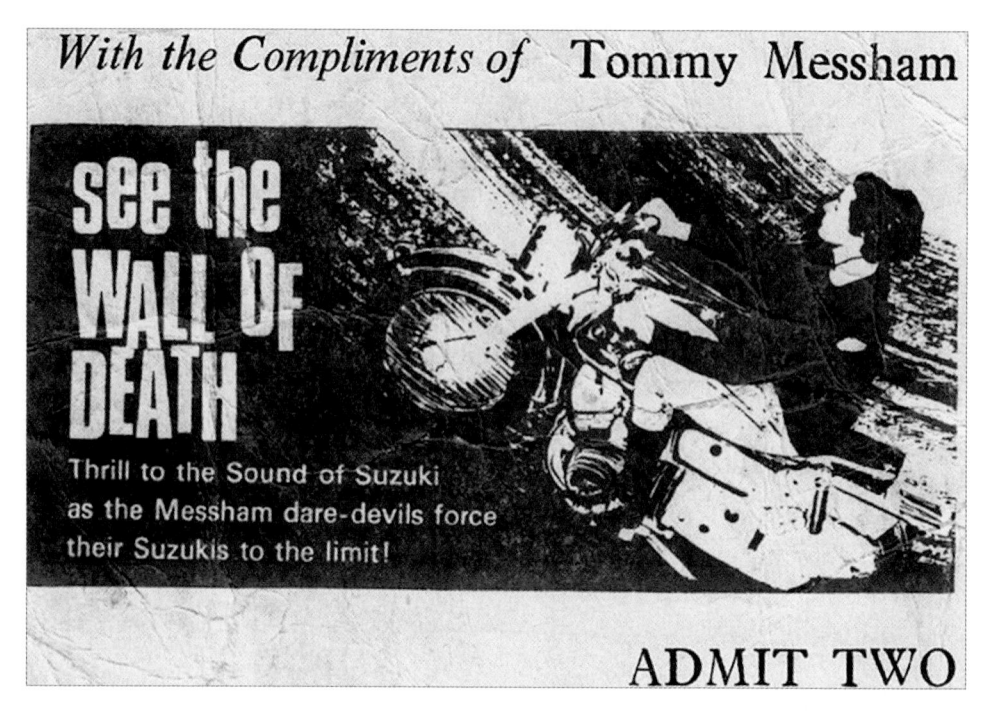

Thrill to the Sound of Suzuki as the Messham dare-devils force their Suzukis to the limit!

ADMIT TWO

Ticket to Tommy Messham's show, 1970s.

Eventually Ford was able to get up on the bottom part of the Wall and decided what he needed was a proper Wall bike. This he achieved by building one based on a Bantam as there were plenty of parts available at the time and they had the advantage of being cheap. Some years later this Bantam was restored by bike engineer Kip Green, although rebuilt is probably a more accurate description given its condition at the time. Ford was to become a stalwart of Messham's show and his subsequent career forms an important part of this story as it unfolds in the following chapter.

Other riders with a link to the Messhams included Doug Murphy, featured in the previous chapter, Peter Catchpole and Jimmy Kynaston, whose stories are intertwined. Peter Catchpole was perhaps one of the most colourful, if not notorious, characters in the post-war Wall story. Trained, fittingly perhaps, by Tornado Smith, Catchpole went on to make a lot of money in property in the Merseyside area, but he never quite got the Wall of Death bug out of his system. His involvement with key individuals such as Yvonne Stagg and Ken Fox will be chronicled later in this story, but some of the shades that made up that colourful personality are worth looking at here.

Catchpole had a habit of turning up at key points in the Wall's history from the 1950s onwards, although disappearing was another of his specialities. After leaving Tornado Smith and riding with Jake Messham, as well as some riding in Germany,

IN THE BLOOD

Boards from the front of Messham's Wall, last opened at Southsea.

Peter Catchpole along with Maureen Swift and Jimmy Kynaston at Munich, 1955.

Jimmy Kynaston on his trick bike. (Messham Archive)

where he was well known by the middle of the decade, he had his own Wall at New Brighton. On one occasion he was riding this and noticed that there was a gap in the crowd along the top of the walkways. He finished his show and came down, only to discover that part of the outside of the Wall had collapsed, taking its audience with it. This was one of the many occasions in his career when he made a hasty exit.

As has already been mentioned many riders regard Kynaston as the best they've ever seen for trick riding, although Kynaston wasn't his real name. No one in the Wall community ever knew what he had been born as, the name Jimmy Kynaston being taken from a headstone because he liked the sound of it. This change had been forced due to the fact that he'd been a deserter during the Second World War and he'd needed a change of identity. A striking figure, tall, blond and good-looking, Kynaston was another stunt rider in *The Wall of Death* and struck up a friendship with Doug Murphy in the early 1950s that the latter never forgot, Kynaston's name later being painted on the side of his revered bike in his memory. Kynaston's end did not befit his iconic status. Having finished with Jake Messham and following some riding in Germany, he went out to Sierra Leone with fellow riders Yvonne Stagg and Doug Oliver, led by Peter Catchpole, who had reappeared after losing some of his audience at New Brighton, bringing that Wall with him. Catchpole already had good contacts in Western Africa, having been paid by the Nigerian government to take a funfair to

IN THE BLOOD

Lagos to celebrate their independence in 1960. The funfair included a boxing booth, Wall of Death, several rides and The Great Leone and his bendy pole act. This then moved on to Freetown in Sierra Leone where Catchpole thought he could make it pay. He was wrong. The Wall was not a big success and it was taken down and put into storage by Stagg, although she never told anyone where she put it and its location was a secret she took with her to her grave. After a spell of diamond prospecting, using the generators to drive a vacuum pump to suck up silt from a river bed, the three riders were left stranded and Kynaston had to take a job in a garage where he developed a duodenal ulcer. With no money to treat him, his colleagues were left powerless as they watched Kynaston deteriorate and eventually die, with Oliver left with the thankless task of burying his former colleague.

One factor in Catchpole's favour was that he was an excellent rider. He could do a side stand on the pedals with a six-inch gap between him and the machine. He was also the one man ever to master Tornado Smith's Loop the Loop. It was no surprise therefore when he reappeared in 1975 after building up an empire in amusements alongside his property interests. He had sensed an opportunity to buy Tornado Smith's old Wall off Yvonne Stagg and her Austrian partner Gustav Kokos, which they were running in Margate. Kokos had joined Stagg in 1967 from

Yvonne Stagg trick riding a BSA at Southend.

Germany, where he had been riding the Wall. Yvonne Stagg had begun riding at the Festival of Britain in Battersea in 1951, where she was working as a rock seller to supplement her income as a secretary. Fascinated with the Wall, she persuaded Frank Todd, whose Wall was a prominent attraction, to take her up on the handlebars and before long she'd been taken on as part of the team, bitten by the bug. She stayed with Todd after the festival, touring England and Scotland through 1952 before joining Francis Manders' Wall of Death and linking up later on with Kitty Mathieu in Germany, a recurring figure and something of a legend in her own right in the story of the Wall.

Stagg's involvement with Tornado Smith has already been mentioned, riding the Southend Wall in the summer and spending her winters in West Africa. After buying Smith's Wall off him in 1965 Stagg became one of the Wall's most prominent figures, her looks and readiness with a quote making her a favourite with newspaper reporters. With the closure of the Kursaal Stagg moved to Dreamland in Margate, initially operating with two BSA Star twins. It wouldn't have been a proper Wall show without Indians though and, after a while, one found its way to her via Australia from her old friend, post-war rider Harry Holland, who sent it to her 'with a big kiss', because he wanted it to be ridden and cherished as he had. Things initially went well at Margate as Stagg settled down with her partner Kokos, and she had a baby girl, Minka. In an interview with a national newspaper in 1970, when she was thirty, Stagg was quoted as saying 'I can't imagine myself a housewife at home all day with kids hanging around my apron.' Perhaps it was this determination not to succumb to the 'normal' – many women riders had given up to raise a family – that explained why her life became more complicated as the decade unfolded.

Around the same time as Catchpole reappeared in the mid-1970s, Stagg went back to the house she shared with Kokos in Southend at the end of the season, leaving her partner behind to carry out some maintenance on a go-kart track he also owned. Stagg took up with a lover, and at the same time became more and more dependent on drink. When word of the lover got back to Kokos he downed tools and went back to sort things out. The man in question, Terry Biebuyck, was waiting for Kokos and stabbed him to death, the subsequent trial providing lurid national front-page news amid allegations that Kokos had beaten Stagg. Biebuyck got a relatively light three-year sentence for manslaughter, having been acquitted of murder, and Stagg vowed to wait for him. Her descent into drink became steeper, however, and she committed suicide over the New Year of 1976/77, her body lying undiscovered for a number of days. This was the end of a sad tale, with Stagg having become an increasing liability on the Wall in the months before and also being involved in a bad car accident in the August of 1976 when she broke a leg, wrist and several ribs after hitting a railway bridge in Margate while under the influence.

IN THE BLOOD

Above: Yvonne Stagg's Wall, now at Dreamland, Margate 1975.

Right: Poster advertising the Wall at Dreamland, 1974.

RIDING THE WALL OF DEATH

In the year between these two deaths Peter Catchpole had bought Stagg's Wall, riding it alongside Allan Ford. Catchpole was full of grand plans around this time, of taking the Wall to Australia and giving Stagg the opportunity to build a new life. Although Stagg was destined not to cross the world, Catchpole ended up fulfilling this ambition, although as we shall see it wasn't a very happy experience.

Yet another character worthy of mention from around this time, who had also enjoyed a spell with Tommy Messham, was the Russian rider Sergei Chityan. An air of Cold War mystery surrounds this individual, who rode in Britain in the early 1980s but also spent time working with the Varanne brothers in France. Rumours seemed to crystallise around Chityan like ice round metal, not least due to his fondness for taking photographs, and not always of obvious targets, with steelworks a favourite. One version of his story said that he was trained by the State in Russia and he earned his spurs travelling from town to town around the Eastern Bloc, where he would travel alone, not with a fair, in order to provide entertainment for the workers. He was trained to such a degree that he could start the bike up, take his hands from the handlebars, go onto the Wall and do all his tricks without touching the handlebars once. That was his act, however, exactly the same every time, no showmanship or smiles, more of a humourless display of technical excellence in keeping with the dark and threatening times. Chityan rode with both Albert Evans, where he continued his habit of disappearing with his camera during the week, on one occasion vanishing to South Africa for a whole summer; as well as with Tommy Messham, during which time he was briefly in police custody, although no charges were ever pressed.

In the winter of 1981 Chityan built his own Wall in a Fulham builder's yard using, it was said, some superb wood supplied direct from Russia. This he transported to Aberavon in Wales for completion, incorporating some old house stairs he found in a demolition yard. He was approached by the showman Pat Evans and subsequently took his Wall to Porthcawl for a season, although the Wall never acquired a tilt and could only be ridden in good weather. After this Chityan vanished to Africa, where he briefly bumped into Peter Catchpole, provoking a confrontation. Whether he was made a better offer by another showman or by his masters we shall never know.

To conclude this chapter it is necessary to mention another family whose name has already featured in this story and to provide a final example of how the Wall gets into the blood: the Cripseys. Roy Cripsey was another early Wall rider and, after travelling with a Wall, settled down with a static one in Skegness. From here he trained up his sons Graham and Gary, who ran the Wall after their father died of emphysema, a common Wall rider's complaint that also accounted for Jake Messham and Doug Murphy's deaths, eventually pulling the Wall down in 1982 in common with the trend at that time.

IN THE BLOOD

Above left: Peter Catchpole with Maureen Swift, Jimmy Kynaston and Siggi Sluppke on the new BMW R25s.

Above right: Sergei Chityan at Queen's Hall Christmas Fair, Leeds in 1983.

Sign advertising Sergei's Wall, featuring 'The Great Russian'.

RIDING THE WALL OF DEATH

A young Ken Fox riding side saddle.

Roy Cripsey also trained up Ken Fox, whose family had been running a shooting attraction and were known to the Cripseys. Ken started as young as thirteen at the cash box and within two years was riding. In another example of the ever-decreasing circle surrounding the Wall around this time Ken joined Peter Catchpole in his Australian adventure, although this tour ended in financial disaster, offering Catchpole another cue to disappear just after the Wall burned down in mysterious circumstances, leaving Fox to sell the BSAs they'd come out with and work his passage back to England.

Graham Cripsey went on to become a professional snooker player and Gary to run a pub, but they had been bitten, it was in their blood, and they were back in the late 1990s with another Wall, bought off Tommy Messham junior, proving once again the tight-knit nature of the Wall of Death community. It seemed that snooker hadn't provided the same level of thrills as the Wall and Graham Cripsey soon started cropping up in the newspapers with his new female rider Vicky Bonnett, an ex-nanny, and his nine-year-old daughter Frankie. The bug was being passed to the next generation.

By way of a postscript to this chapter, in 2004 Alma Skinner, whose Wall riding career was featured in an earlier chapter, by then aged ninety-four, was taken to Ken Fox's Wall when it visited Stoke-on-Trent. For the first time in her life she watched the show from the walkrounds – and was terrified! She declared she much preferred to be inside or preferably on the Wall. The bug had never left her and she had to be talked out of being taken up on the Wall on Ken's handlebars.

EIGHT

LAST CHANCE TO SEE... ?

By the mid-1980s, anyone wanting to see a Wall of Death in Britain would have been disappointed. Not a single operating Wall remained. Although there were still a handful scattered about they tended to be in showmen's yards or, worse, lying unprotected in the open slowly rotting away.

This was the situation in Britain at least – stories continued to circulate of Walls popping up in far-away places such as Russia, which seems to have had a continuing fascination with the Wall, and where there was a concrete Wall for a while in Gorky Park, as well as India, Holland and Australia, Denmark and several still in Germany – with Walls still a feature at the Munich Oktoberfest, Hamburg Domfest and Stuttgart Volksfest. The handful of British riders still earning their living from the Wall had been forced to pack up their bikes and try their luck abroad or find something new to do. One such was the ex-Messham rider Allan Ford, who had bought a house in Reigate during his last season riding in Margate during 1977. This represented a return to his roots, his father having run an antique watch and clock restoration business in Deal, and perhaps an acknowledgement that the time had come to settle down. There were simply no more Walls left to ride.

First, however, there was the opportunity for one last adventure. Through a contact at Dreamland he heard of a contract in Iran. He went for lunch to an Iranian restaurant in South Kensington to see what was needed and, following the meal, Ford flew out to Tehran, never having even been abroad before, and spent the night at the home of his contact, an amusement park operator who couldn't speak a word of English, but enjoyed the benefit of having six wives. The next day they drove down the country to Messhad, the capital of the province of Khorasan on the Afghan border in north-east Iran. A Holy City, Messhad had an amusement park where pilgrims spent their free time. Here Ford noticed a Wall, his first clue as to why he was there, of Italian construction that, it turned out, had previously been ridden by a Turkish rider who went by the name of Can Oriel, whose other speciality was to ride a motorbike on its rims along a steel cable strung out across the top of the park.

The Wall wasn't totally vertical and, although the riding surface was wooden, it was made out of tubular steel. Along with all the other attractions on the park the Wall carried a picture of the doomed Shah and his sons on top of its centre pole. Luckily the manager of the park used to run the Hilton Hotel in Messhad and spoke English. A thoroughly enjoyable three months followed during which time Ford rode some ancient CZ two-stroke bikes, so decrepit the canvas was showing through on their tyres. The Wall itself got hot and dusty and was hosed down once a day in the morning. The crowds were big and Ford was able to give them a decent show, although being on his own he was naturally limited in what he could do. Their society was on the brink of major change; women were just beginning to show themselves in public and the people were so poor they were happy when the top prize on a side stall was a sachet of shampoo, but like people everywhere the Iranian people still had the capacity to be thrilled by the Wall.

His adventure over, on his return Ford succumbed to the need to live a normal life and bought a lawnmower repair business. The previous summer had been so dry that the previous owner of the business had gone bust. Ford had a small workshop in his back yard and was good with machinery so, like many other riders around this time, he reconciled himself to a new life. He built the business up and started to employ people, but the Wall was in his blood. Ford kept in touch with the fairground world through *World's Fair* and, in 1985, he spotted a Wall for sale. It just so happened that Customs & Excise had been on strike that year and Ford was sitting on some cash kept aside to pay his VAT. The temptation was irresistible. He went up to Skegness to see the Wall. It was the one previously run by the Cripsey family, and a price was agreed. The Wall was kept in some sheds and it was difficult to assess its condition, but it was the only one available and by that time he'd warmed to the idea of owning a Wall of his own. The deed done, Ford had to pull together an army of people, buy a rusty old articulated lorry and find a driver. Within a few weeks the Wall was back in Reigate and it was possible to see just how bad a condition it was in. Using his mower business staff and calling on friends, Ford restored the Wall in his spare time, the whole thing taking around a year, and trialled it at a steam rally at Blindley Heath near Godstone.

By this time the public had been denied the chance to see a Wall in action for a few years and had an appetite for the thrills it could offer. Ford's timing was also good in that the economy was picking up after a period in the doldrums. An era of champagne and yuppies, of people feeling positive and having more money in their pockets, had just dawned. Things went well for the Wall and Ford reinvested all he could in the business, now called The Motordrome Company (slogan: 'We Get Around To It'), at one point buying the Atkinson lorry that had once transported Malcolm Campbell's 'Bluebird', allowing this adventurer a second appearance in the Wall's history.

LAST CHANCE TO SEE... ?

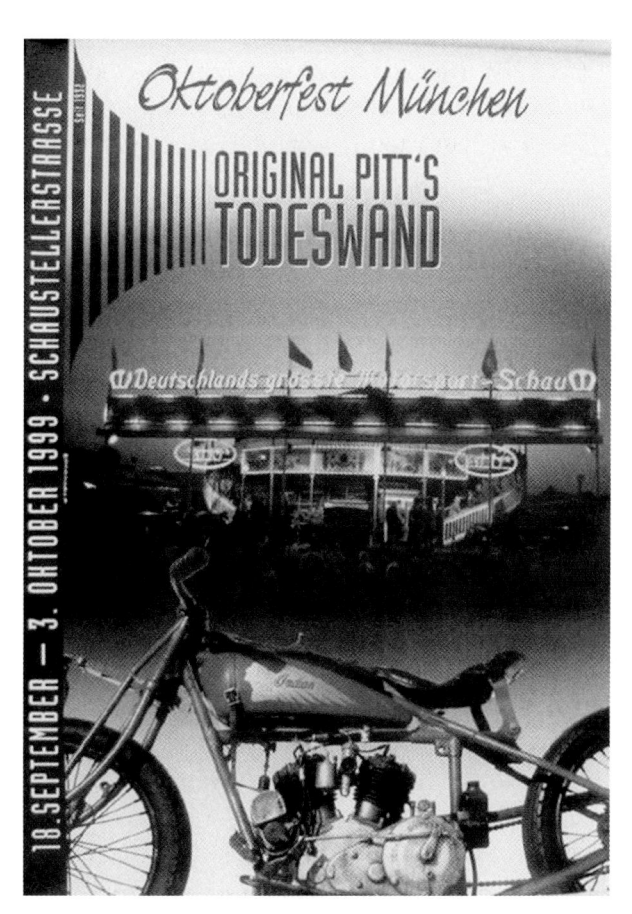

Right: Poster advertising Pitt's Todeswand or Wall of Death, 1999.

Below: Ticket to the Varannes' show in France.

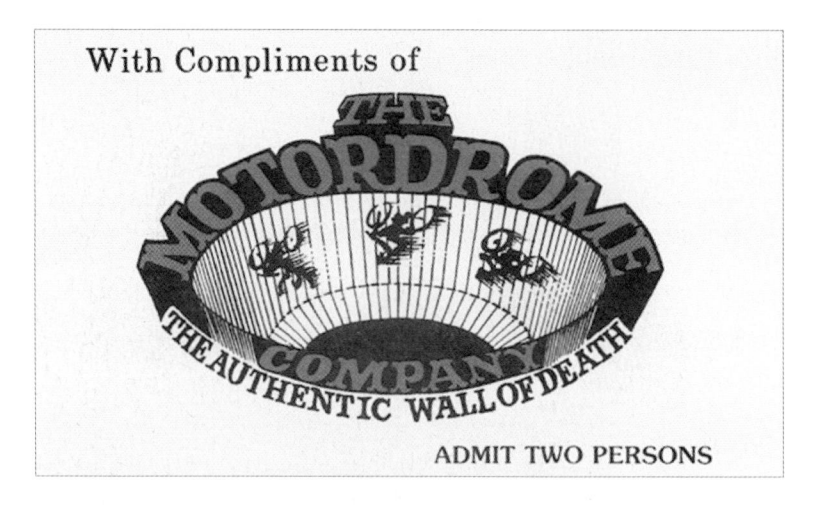

Ticket to the Motordrome Company show, 1990s.

Allan Ford warming up the crowd on the rollers before a show.

LAST CHANCE TO SEE... ?

Motordrome after a muddy Kent Custom Show.

For a couple of seasons Ford had the fairgrounds to himself, but word soon got around and the reservoir of interest in the Wall of Death that lay just below the surface found a way through. Although the activity that followed wasn't a fountain, it was a significant flow. Predictably perhaps, Peter Catchpole's face was among the first to emerge. After a couple of years in west Africa, Ken Fox reappeared with Catchpole's Wall, or a version of it made using salvaged parts of Tornado Smith's old Wall, at Southport. This was not in a good condition though, and its tilt had been blown off in a storm. Fox was clearly struggling to make ends meet, and before long Catchpole sold the Wall to the Buxworth Steam Group, who had ambitions to create a fully comprehensive travelling steam fair operation.

Ford had demonstrated the popularity of a Wall at steam fairs, and as this was Buxworth's core market, having their own Wall must have seemed like a good idea. At the time the company was spending money freely, buying the Iron Maiden traction engine as well as investing heavily in all parts of their business. Although good in theory, the idea didn't work out quite as well in practice and the group, under the leadership of the two Marchington brothers, struggled. Before long there was a parting of the ways and Tony Marchington, who had initially made his money out of pharmaceuticals, went off to buy the Flying Scotsman steam train. The financial demands of this enterprise led to the sale of most of Buxworth's assets, although the Wall of Death was bought by Tony Marchington's brother who still owns it today, along with panels from Tornado Smith's original Wall.

Fox at last gravitated to Ford's Motordrome Company in 1990, riding with him until 1992. By this time Ford's Motordrome Company was acting as a honeypot for riders old and new. One of these was Gerry de Roy, who at that time was the oldest Wall rider in the country, and another was Chris Lee, another

RIDING THE WALL OF DEATH

Ken Fox in action with the Motordrome Company.

Tommy Messham-trained rider who had become a train driver when the Walls had disappeared. Ford also trained up new riders, most significantly Ned Kelly, a former despatch rider from Wales who stayed with Ford for a number of years, along with Ken De wolf, Geoff Allen, Gary Sykes and Rob Richardson.

Lee had joined Messham around the same time as Ford himself, in the early 1970s and stayed with him for ten years, interspersed by spells in Germany. In an article on the Wall in 1977, the *Evening Standard* described Lee as looking the part with 'dyed, ginger swept-up hair, tattoos, six gold rings in his left ear... the expression on his face scornful, conveying that he knows he is frightening his audience more than he is frightening himself.'[27] In 1975 Lee managed to beat 'Speedy' Babbs' world endurance record for riding the Wall in Dublin, going round for three-and-a-half hours, although in a stroke of bad luck his feat was never officially acknowledged as that year one of the two editors of the *Guinness Book of Records*, Ross McWhirter, was murdered, leading to confusion over that year's entries. Lee's time was subsequently beaten in 1982 by a German, Hugo Dabbert at Russelsheim, who rode for 6,841 laps on a 32-foot Wall for over six hours.

LAST CHANCE TO SEE...?

In carrying out his day job after leaving Messham Chris Lee spotted Ford's Wall built up at Battersea, where they were recording a Channel 4 documentary, and used to toot his whistle every time he went past. In the end he rode down to see Ford and ended up riding with him whenever he could.

Ned Kelly, real name Neil Smart, joined Allan Ford in the late 1980s after Ford had taken Kelly's girlfriend up on the Wall and the pair got talking. A despatch rider at the time, Kelly's greatest asset was that he held an HGV licence, something Ford was in desperate need of, and he agreed to join the Motordrome Company and to learn how to ride the Wall. A quick learner, Kelly remained with Ford the following winter as they refurbished the Wall in the old Officers' Mess at Santa Pod. He learned to trick ride the following season and rode on and off with Ford over the next ten years, also enjoying a spell in Germany with Ken Fox.

Steam fairs continued to provide the mainspring of Ford's business, but it was far from easy work or money. One explanation for the decline in the number of Walls in the 1970s had been the sense that their time had passed. Their accent on showmanship and focus on old motorbikes had made them seem as if they belonged

When two Walls met – The Ken Fox Troupe and the Motordrome Company, Great Dorset Steam Fair 1998. From left to right: Chris Lee, Kerry Ann, Allan Ford, Ken Fox, Gerry de Roy, Danny Dare and a German rider.

to a different era. At a time when most fairground attractions were trying their best to link into the modern pop culture an emphasis on pre-war riding heroes and motorbikes seemed almost quaint. Walls of Death seemed equally out of step in terms of their set up. Most attractions had become leaner in terms of the horse and manpower needed to take them around the country, but the fundamentals of operating a Wall had remained the same since they'd first begun to tour half a century before and this worked against making them viable.

In order to get an idea of the intensity of effort required to keep a Wall of Death show on the road, consider the schedule of a 'typical' week, during which the Wall might have been presented at a steam rally. The working week tended to start on a Monday with the day spent travelling from one gaff to the next and the night spent in a lay-by or other known spot as close as possible to the next destination. Either Monday night or Tuesday morning a car would be taken to find the next site in order to avoid the possibility of getting lost with the train of five or six vehicles, including a 40-foot articulated truck, a seven-and-a-half-ton box lorry, a HIAB lorry, a transit van and a car — each pulling a caravan — down what might be poor access. Once the site was found the Wall would be allocated its position by the riding master, the man with responsibility for telling each attraction where it went. As a Wall was usually seen as a crowd-puller this was likely to be a good spot, which was just as well as there was often very little room for negotiation with these hard men. The car would then return to the wagons and the whole train brought in. The next important step would be to establish a base, so the caravans, or living wagons, could be sited and levelled.

If it was still morning a start might then be made on the build — erecting the Wall itself. The first, absolutely critical task, one that wasn't worth hurrying, would be to determine where the centre would go. If this was wrong by half an inch the whole Wall would be a couple of feet out by the time it was up, possibly enough to infringe on another attraction's 'ground' and even, in a worst-case situation, require a dismantling and restart of the build, something everyone would want to avoid. Finding the centre could be done with a tape measure, but another trick was to have a piece of rope set out in a triangle with four knots in it setting out the position of the corners of the entrance and exit stairs, the centre of the 'front' and the centre of the Wall itself, a sort of mini-template. The centre would then be laid, literally a circular piece of wood probably no more than a couple of feet in diameter with hinges around its circumference from which sleepers would in time radiate out. With the centre laid the head gaffer would then test the wind direction, with the aim of having the wind at the back of the first panels so he could rope them if necessary. The final crucial consideration would be the lie of the land. Was it flat or on a slope? If there was a slope then the build needed to begin with the sleeper which would need the least 'packing' or blocks of wood laid under it in order to

Pushing up the panels during a build-up.

ensure the whole construction sat on the level, the first sleeper acting as a datum point for those that followed. If there was a pronounced slope it might even have been necessary to dig some sleepers in, in order to avoid the need for too much packing of lower sleepers later on in the process. The first sleeper was attached to the centre and levelled throughout its length, again a task that required absolute precision with time spent on getting this right always time well spent. As such, a good spirit level was an essential tool, and this would be used to get the centre to the same level as the sleeper, packing it if necessary.

When all the sleepers were down they would be checked again with the spirit level, turned each way, the construction now beginning to look like a child's drawing of a sun, with solid rays emanating from the centre. There were four critical load bearing points on each sleeper, one where the panels sat on the outside, one where the track met the floor, one where the bikes stood and another at the very end, and these would determine where the packing went. Once the sleepers had been set out to everyone's satisfaction the floor could be laid. Depending on the vehicles, the floor timbers would either be manhandled off the wagon or, if they were lucky, craned down. Either way, this was a labour-intensive part of the exercise, usually requiring a minimum of four people. It is likely that the opportunity would also be taken at this stage to unload the gates and with these all off the wagons this would be a good time to pause both for lunch and to take breath, and to check that everything was going to plan and looked okay.

After lunch the process of getting the first of the panels up began. Two gates would be manhandled upright and, meanwhile, side panels would be craned off the wagon and up to the side of the Wall, resting on the ground. At this point the importance of packing away to a pattern that took the build into account would come into play as it was important to have the door panel available – the gaffers didn't want to find out that it was at the bottom of the pile when they needed it. The top panel would then be taken and a man put on each corner. One man would then go up behind and put his feet at the base of the panel while the other three literally pushed the panel up. The man who had been at the back then climbed up the panel and dropped a locating pin into place. The first panel would now be up, but there was no time for the lads to stop and admire their handiwork as this would represent one of the most dangerous points in the build. A rogue gust of wind would see the panel acting as a sail, sending it over and possibly on top of anyone who happened to be in the way. One precaution therefore might be to tie a rope from the top of the panel to one of the wagons just in case.

The process would then be repeated, pinning as they went, with the Wall beginning by now to take on a familiar shape, until the men got to the final panel. This had to go up from the outside. It's possible that the banking track would now be carried inside the Wall while there was still plenty of space and, once the final panel was in place, cables would be stretched around the Wall to make it safe – at this stage pulled hand tight.

By this time everyone would probably have had enough and it would be time to stop for the day. With some luck it may rain overnight, which tended to wash the dust away and swell the panels up so they become tighter. Work began the next day with the walkrounds and handrails, which would be on the top of the load on the wagons and therefore close to hand. These would be followed in turn by the stairs, which tended to come as complete units rather than in sections and, as such, were very heavy, requiring a rope to pull them up where they would be hooked up at the top.

The next stage to getting the Wall into a recognisable form was to get the centre pole and tilt, or canopy, up, along with the roundings or side panels. The front followed, which may have come in sections or may have been in a trailer in its own right, along with the electrics. The Wall would now be up and, although easy to describe the process, it's difficult to appreciate the sheer back-busting effort involved unless you were one of the participants. Even though they had the assistance of gaff-lads when it came to the heavy manual labour, riders would be expected to get stuck in and would often find themselves exhausted before they'd even begun to ride.

In a schedule such as this Thursday would tend to be set aside for any maintenance, be it on bikes, wagons or generators or even tasks as basic as replacing blown bulbs. If time permitted, novices might even be allowed a bit of training and the riders

LAST CHANCE TO SEE... ?

The Motordrome convoy on its way to Hull, 1991.

may indulge in a little practice, just to make sure the Wall was riding okay. There may even be an inspection at this point from the health and safety people. Friday was utility day when washing, shopping and the other basic chores of day-to-day living got done and, depending upon the type of event, there may even be a couple of shows, for example for those camping at a rally.

Saturday and Sunday were the big days when the riding actually got done. Shows tended to start around 11 a.m. and went on into the evening, the number of shows per hour depending upon the popularity of the event and in turn of the Wall. Sundays tended to be the bigger day at a steam rally, but these also ended earlier. As the last show came to its conclusion the process of pulling down would begin – some of the peripheral fittings may even have been taken down as last show was underway. Ideally, before the day was out, the bikes would be loaded away, the tilt and electrics brought down and the top stripped off, leaving the panels standing, with the aim of finishing around 10 p.m. Depending on how far the wagons had to get the next day, Monday, the chaps would be turned out of their kip trucks and the rest of the pull down completed although, if the weather was bad or if it wasn't possible to pull onto the next gaff until Wednesday, there might be the chance to linger.

The effort remained the same each time, but the takings could vary enormously, as could the experience. Bad weather not only made the whole build a miserable job but kept the crowds away. There were few things more dispiriting than going through the physical demands of a build in the full knowledge that the weekend was

RIDING THE WALL OF DEATH

Above: The Motordrome Wall loaded up and ready to go.

Left: A modern poster advertising a Wall at the Munich Oktoberfest, 1998.

Deutschlands größte Motorsport - Schau

auf der Wies'n zum Münchner Oktoberfest
in der Schausteller - Straße
(19.09. - 04.10.1998)

Erleben Sie das
abenteuerliche Vergnügen
mit Darbietungen der
Steilwandfahrer
"Motodrome Company"
aus England

likely to be poor. Equally, no two grounds were ever the same. The ground may be flat or sloping, hard, soft or even tarmac. The people might be friendly or hostile, the 'company' willing or unavailable, but one thing most of those involved would agree on – most times it beat working nine to five in an office.

Ford's was not the only revival around this time, with a similar story unfolding across the Atlantic. In 1979 American Wall rider Wayne Campbell bought the Wall he'd previously ridden from 1972 to 1976 when it had been owned by Joe Boudreau of Ocean Grove, Massachusetts. Boudreau in turn had had it built in 1962 in order to replace one his father had originally constructed in 1929. The Wall came complete with eight Indian Scouts, four being 37-cubic-inch models made between 1924 and 1927, the others being 45-cubic-inch 1928 models. After two years' restoration work, mainly spent on the bikes, although the Wall itself had needed six inches of rotten wood to be cut off all the way round, the Wall went out on the road.

Elsewhere Walls continued to refuse to die, with reports resurfacing of the concrete Wall in Gorky Park in Russia, as well as others in Australia, Dubai, Thailand, India, Holland and Denmark. Interest also continued in Britain, and it began to seem as if Ford's view, once expressed in a magazine article that 'we are the last of the dinosaurs really' was about to be proved wrong. Towards the end of the 1980s Ford was approached to see if he wanted to buy Albert Evans' old Wall. Demand for the show remained strong and Ford quite fancied the idea of being a big-time showman with two travelling Walls and took up the offer. If nothing else, he rationalised, buying the Wall eliminated a potential source of competition and the clincher was the fact that Evans' Wall came with a couple of Indians, which would be useful.

This time Ford's timing was less inspired. Even though interest in motorbikes was again on the rise, accompanied by a growing number of custom bike shows, which were natural territory for Walls, the economy was once again heading into recession and people had less money jangling in their pockets. Costs went up while income went down.

If the physical demands of building a Wall had changed very little since the 1930s, the economics of running one certainly had, making it harder to keep a Wall on the road and making a poor weekend an even harder blow to take. The cost of fuel alone continued to rise; diesel for the wagons and petrol for the lorries, generators and bikes these days can account for at least £500 a week, a figure that's bound to continue to outstrip inflation. To that must be added the rent for the sites as well as wages and insurance. One of the steepest increases in more liability-conscious times has been insurance premiums, with proprietors required to carry as much as £10 million liability in some cases, with premiums high not least because there's such a narrow base to spread the risk, and there's employer's liability insurance on top of that – the days of the anonymous roustabout have become a distant memory.

RIDING THE WALL OF DEATH

As might be expected the regulatory environment also tightened considerably in the 1990s. Showmen used to get concessions on their vehicles, most of which went. These included the length of vehicle they could take out on The Queen's highway and the type of fuel they could use. The days when showmen might use cheaper pink agricultural diesel also disappeared, as had cheaper vehicle licences on the basis that showmen were only travelling short distances from fair to fair, something that no longer held true. One concession that did remain, however, is the one that allowed showmen to be the only people who can pull two trailers, a right that was originally granted as they used to be driven by steam and one vehicle had to pull a water carrier.

To all this had to be added the running costs of the Wall itself, the requirement to replace the tilt probably every five years, the need to keep a yard where the Wall could pull over in the winter, ideally with some kind of shed where maintenance could be carried out, and the costs began to spiral even before the fixed costs of tax, accountancy, caravans, vehicle maintenance and depreciation were taken into account.

By the late 1980s, running a travelling Wall of Death was a delicate balancing act. Choosing the right places to go, getting the advance publicity right and making sure you have a top-notch spieler had become at least as important as the skills of the riders, even though they often had to be combined in the same individual. Having family prepared to ride or run the cash box became almost a requirement, so tight had margins become. At the same time income had become precarious, varying greatly depending on the weather, whether the local paper picked up on your story, the mood the crowd was in and whether people had seen the show before. Choosing the right event became an art – steam fair or bike show? Traditional event or a new one with potential?

Despite all this others were prepared to give it a shot and, notwithstanding Ford's attempts to stifle the competition, other Walls began to emerge onto the scene, not all of them successfully. After a spell helping to run his father-in-law's arcade business, Tommy Messham junior, who had married within the Guild, had one last go at exorcising the Wall bug from his blood. In 1994 he restored a Wall and took it to Singapore, but the trip was less than successful and, after a season in Ireland, he finally gave up the ghost, selling the Wall to the Cripsey family.

Graham Cripsey picked up the Wall in Dublin and took it to Skegness, recruiting a female rider and ex-nanny called Vicky Bonnett from an advertisement in a newsagent's window. Despite never haven ridden a bike before, she was selected on the basis that she smiled as she went round the Wall and gave off an air of charisma.[28] Graham Cripsey continued to tour his Wall the following season, including a pitch at the *Motorcycle News* Butlin's weekend in 1997, although to nothing like the schedule followed by Ford at the time.

Peter Catchpole had already rebuilt a version of Tornado Smith's Wall, the one he'd sold to the Buxford Steam Group, but in doing so he'd attempted to have a trailer-mounted

The Ken Fox Troupe, 2005, with fairground historian Neil Calladine speiling.

floor, which made it smaller, something which hadn't been a big success. Undeterred, he worked with Ken Fox to build two further Walls, one of them at the old Harland and Wolff shipyard in Merseyside, the same place where Polaris submarines had been built and where Tommy Messham's Globe had originally been built. The first of these went on to travel as The Ken Fox Troupe and was until recently the only travelling Wall of Death, having picked up that particular mantle from Allan Ford who'd finally pulled in in 2000 after acquiring a pub and falling victim to the appalling weather that began the season that year. Peter Catchpole died at the same time, at which point Ken Fox became sole owner of his Wall, which he travels along with his wife, who operates the cash box, and his son Luke, riding alongside a young female rider Kerri Cameron.

Before finally pulling in Allan Ford was destined to go out on a high, although he wasn't to know it was to be his last season at the time. Encouraged by promoter Godfrey Spargo, Ford agreed to build his Wall up on the car park of the White Hart in Boxford, Suffolk, the pub once owned by Tornado Smith's parents and regarded by some as the spiritual home of the Wall of Death. Ford had arrived with low expectations, content that the stop was on the way to the more important Henham Steam Rally near Southwold. Spargo, however, had excelled himself in the publicity he'd generated and people started to emerge from nowhere, on tractors, in buses, on

RIDING THE WALL OF DEATH

Above left: Gerry de Roy on the rollers – he is in the *Guinness Book of Records* as the world's oldest Wall rider.

Above right: Exposed to the elements and rotting away – Allan Ford's old Wall.

trailers. The interest was almost overwhelming and the whole event turned out to be seminal. Even Tornado Smith's younger brother Basil turned up. Ford rode alongside his colleagues Gerry de Roy, Chris Lee and Ken Wolf, with Gerry, by then seventy-two years old, having had the distinction of riding with Tornado himself in the late 1950s, adding further to a general air of 'fin de siecle'. Unlike Lee, de Roy had made it into the *Guinness Book of Records* for endurance of a different kind – as the oldest Wall of Death rider. Numerous Boxford residents rode on one of the sets of handlebars during the Wall's visit, including the pub landlord's fourteen-year-old twin sons who wore lion costumes throughout in memory of Smith's Briton, and during the weekend Ford gave illustrated talks on the history of the Wall. It was to be a good way to bow out.

Sadly, both of Ford's Walls have met undignified ends. His main Wall was sold to a Cornish couple who intended to run it as a business. Unfortunately they broke up soon after buying the Wall and it is thought to be rotting away exposed to the elements somewhere in that county and, after all this time, it is extremely unlikely that it will be salvageable. A similar fate befell his second Wall, the one that once belonged to both Albert Evans and Tommy Messham, which is currently sitting in a

LAST CHANCE TO SEE... ?

Charles Winter with James Messham and son Nathan.

Chris Palmer's Wall, the ex-Cripsey Wall of Fear, Horndean, 2005.

An American 'Widow Maker' Wall, also rotting away in the 1980s. (Copyright Charles Winter)

showman's yard in Sussex and has also probably passed the point at which it could be repaired. Its fate probably lies in flames.

Even though Ken Fox had had the country to himself for a while, like Ford's Motordrome Company it was destined not to last. Over the last decade there seems to be a rule that says there's certainly room for one Wall of Death possibly two, although the optimum number probably lies somewhere in the middle. Two new contenders emerged onto the scene in 2005, although neither seems to have the ambition to replace the Ken Fox Troupe as the country's leading travelling Wall. There is still at least one traditional Wall out there; appropriately enough perhaps, the one that incorporates parts of Tornado Smith's original Wall and was once owned by the Buxford Steam Group. The first fresh entrant onto the scene is the historic Wall that can list Eddie Monte, Tommy Messham and the Cripseys as its owners, bought in an auction by motorbike enthusiast Chris Palmer in 2005. Palmer has recruited veterans Allan Ford and Chris Lee to ride his Wall on an occasional basis alongside his son Joe and nephew Richard, both of whom have learned the basics and are learning from two masters. Palmer bought the Wall after it failed to meet its reserve at auction, travelling to Skegness to see it. He and his family have subsequently restored it and took it out to a steam fair and the Detling Motorcycle Rally in 2005 where it proved to be an instant hit, with crowds queuing to see it. Palmer uses a team of volunteers to run, transport and erect the 40-ton structure and with this support plans to present at around a dozen shows a year.

Palmer's enthusiasm means that there is now an original 1920s Wall back on the road. What's more, it's a larger Wall than Fox's, which allows for more complex stunt riding. He currently runs a go kart on the Wall and there are plans to add a sidecar, Tornado Smith-style, in due course.

The other fresh Wall is the second one built by Peter Catchpole towards the end of his life, and this has been bought by a name that is synonymous with the Wall – Messham, in this case James Messham, nephew to Tommy Messham senior and son of his brother Edward. This is currently based at Shoreham and is being ridden by Charles Winter, Messham himself and his two sons.

The Wall of Death, it seems, refuses to die. History has shown its attraction to be timeless, with a ready stream of people prepared to come forward to ride it, own it, run it and watch it, whatever the social circumstances of the time. Perhaps the explanation for this is deceptively simple – the Wall gives us a clue to the secret of how to lead a satisfying life. On the Wall, as in life, what goes around comes around, but the most important thing of all is to make sure you're always looking forward.

NINE

PART OF THE CULTURE

Mention has already been made of how the glory days of the pre-war period ended with the Wall of Death playing a significant role in the Ealing Comedy starring George Formby called *Spare a Copper* (directed by John Paddy Carstairs), and how a decade later the prominence of the Wall in popular culture was re-affirmed by a film actually called *The Wall of Death* starring Laurence Harvey and directed by Lewis Gilbert. Originally called 'There is Another Sun', the producers of this film clearly saw the potential of a more enticing title. Two years later a Globe of Death also featured in Cecil B. De Mille's classic *The Greatest Show on Earth*.

The speed and glamour that began to attach itself to motorbikes and their riders made them a natural for the movies, and one of the first Wall riders to appear in one was Skid Skinner in *Money for Speed* (directed by Bernard Vorhaus), which came out in 1933, although this featured speedway rather than the Wall. Incidentally, this film was one of the first to be edited by David Lean, who went on to become a leading light of the UK film industry. *Spare a Copper* represented a natural progression and turned out to be the first in a run of films featuring the Wall, with the movie producers seeming to judge that they could afford to return to the theme around once a decade.

1964 saw the release of *Roustabout* (directed by John Rich), starring perhaps the greatest ever icon of popular culture, Elvis Presley. In this film Elvis plays a maverick singer and biker who hooks up with a carnival, where he works as a handyman and ends up riding a Wall. Perhaps reflecting the lean period the Wall itself was experiencing at the time, the 1970s passed without a Wall-themed film, but the 1980s more than made up for this with two in quick succession. One of these, *Eat the Peach*, picks up where Elvis left off, with the two Irish protagonists watching the King in *Roustabout* and being inspired to build their own Wall as something to do when the Japanese owners of the local factory pull out, leaving them jobless. *Eat the Peach*, directed by Peter Ormrod, was the surprise hit of 1986. The film was

Publicity photograph used for the *Girl on a Motorcycle* documentary, 1995.

Just some of the many T-shirts to have featured the Wall over the years.

described in its publicity as 'About losers who are authentic heroes. The Wall is a metaphor for an attempt to assert identity and express individuality,'[29] a statement that could act as an epitaph for a more than one Wall rider over the decades.

Eat the Peach was in fact inspired by real-life events. When Tommy Messham was in Ireland he came back to his Wall one evening to find two men busy with tape measures taking the dimensions of his Wall, and that had indeed been inspired by *Roustabout*. These two went on to build their own Wall using nothing more sophisticated than shuttering ply and old tree trunks. Trick riding for the film was done by Charles Winter who, in a stroke of luck for the director, bore a startling resemblance to the film's lead actor, with stunts coordinated by the scrambler Dave Bickers.

PART OF THE CULTURE

Above left: Even embroidery has embraced the Wall!

Above right: Pride by William Wharton, perhaps one of the best stories around the Wall of Death.

Children's clockwork toy of the Wall from West Germany, early 1950s.

RIDING THE WALL OF DEATH

Left: A children's story book from 1966.

Below: Recently issued plastic model kit of the Wall, produced in Germany, 2005.

PART OF THE CULTURE

The Wall also featured in the less successful, critically at least, *Wild Geese 2*, directed by Peter Hunt, which came out in 1985 and starred a host of big-name actors such as Laurence Olivier and Edward Fox. Fox was actually a late addition to the cast list, roped in when the actor who portrayed his part in the first film, Richard Burton, died two weeks into filming. The Wall has also featured in song, most memorably perhaps in Richard Thompson's track called, appropriately *The Wall of Death*, also recorded by REM, and in books, including R.F. Delderfield's *The Avenue Goes to War*, about the effects of The Blitz on the inhabitants of a single avenue, and William Wharton's *Pride*, probably the best story ever to feature the Wall of Death. There are even examples of the Wall as toys, puzzles, model kits and even embroidery sets.

The aura of the Wall has also proved to be irresistible to promotional film makers over the years. Tommy Messham was once paid by BP to ride his Wall with posters pasted all over the inside and in 1998 Allan Ford and Chris Lee rode in a pop video for the single *This Feeling* by the band Puressence. As TV became the nation's main source of entertainment it was also inevitable that feature shows such as *Noel Edmunds' Saturday Show*, *Top Gear*, *You Bet!* and *Surprise Surprise!* should all latch onto the Wall's potential.

In 1995 Allan Ford and his Wall was the subject of a half-hour documentary in Channel 4's *Short Stories* series with a film called *Girl on a Motorcycle*. This film told the story of how Ford and Ned Kelly had advertised for a woman prepared to ride the handlebars of their bikes around the Wall in order to add a little glamour to the show. The combination of feminist sensibilities high on the social agenda at the time and the 'what you see is what you get' rawness of Ford and Kelly made for an engaging documentary and it ended up being the most repeated Channel 4 documentary of that year. Ken Fox's Wall has also appeared on ITV's *Heartbeat*, fittingly a 1960s nostalgia drama.

With the current revival of interest in the Wall of Death it can only be a matter of time before some media creative type picks up on its potential and features one in some form of media again. In fact, following the publication of the first edition of this book, one 'media type' did just that! In October 2006 the BBC used the Wall of Death as one of its eight new station identifier sequences used between programmes. All these were based upon a circular theme, so the Wall was an obvious subject. The aim was to show ordinary people doing extraordinary things, so once again the Wall must have come readily to mind. The sequence itself was filmed at Shepperton Studios and was directed by Stuart Douglas. Once again the Ken Fox Troupe starred, performing their stunts in a display that *Ariel*, the BBC in-house magazine, described simply as 'spectacular'.

ENDNOTES

[1] Rodney Dale and Joan Grey, *Edwardian Inventions* (Star Books 1979).
[2] Ibid.
[3] 'The Jones-Hilliard Bicycle Sensation', *The Strand*, July 1902, pp.433-435.
[4] Rodney Dale and Joan Grey, *Edwardian Inventions* (Star Books 1979).
[5] Contemporary account in *Motorcycle Illustrated*.
[6] 'Motor Cycling In Mid-Air', *Motor Cycling*, 18 May 1915.
[7] 'Harry V. Sucher: The Iron Redskin' – quoted by Doug Murphy in *World's Fair*, 28 February 1981.
[8] Official Programme of the 1924 British Empire Exhibition, p.100.
[9] An original of this letter is featured in Neil Calladine's history of the Wall on www.wall-of-death.co.uk
[10] *World's Fair*, June and September 1929.
[11] *World's Fair*, Letters Pages. Undated, 1975. Correspondent George Purser.
[12] *World's Fair*, 15 May 1998.
[13] Radio interview on *Woman's Hour*, BBC Radio 4, 16 December 2004.
[14] Letter from Bill Tayleur to Avril Scott Moncrieff.
[15] *The Evening Chronicle*, 25 June 1930.
[16] Quoted in Opschondek, Dering and Schreiber's *Im Banne Der Motoren*, (Buchendorfer Verlag 1995).
[17] 'Tornado Smith, My Life As A Wall Rider,' *Motor Cycle Magazine*, 4 October 1934.
[18] 'Daring Don Dices With Death,' *Motor Cycling*, 11 May 1961.
[19] *Vintage Spirit*, October 2005.
[20] *World's Fair* Letters Pages. Sept/Oct 1977. Correspondents Frank Newby and Mrs John Sparks.
[21] *World's Fair* Letters Pages. Undated, 1975. Correspondent Sid Bennett.
[22] US Patent 759130, 3 May 1904.
[23] *The Motocycle News*, Vol II, No. 11 April 1909.
[24] According to research by US Drome and Globe rider 'Lucky' Thibeault.
[25] *The Daily Express*, 17 October 1996.
[26] *Sydney Morning Herald*, 22 March 1997.
[27] *Evening Standard*, 15 April 1977.
[28] 'I'll Change Nappies No More,' *The Daily Express*, 23 October 1996.
[29] Quote from synopsis issued by United International Pictures.

WALL OF FAME

This Wall of Fame has been put together to acknowledge those who, over the decades, have made a significant contribution to establishing and maintaining the Wall of Death legend and keeping the show on the road. This Wall includes not just riders but others without whom it may not have become the entertainment icon it is today.

It would of course be impossible to produce a comprehensive list, and the authors apologise in advance to anyone who should be on the list and has somehow been missed off. If you are aware of anyone who you feel should be on the list please get in touch with us through the Allan Ford website and we'll see if they can be included in future editions of this book: www.thewallofdeath.com

PAULETTE AND HENRI ABBINS
An early French pair of Globe of Death riders.

GEOFF ALLEN
The first rider taught to ride by Allan Ford when he revived the Wall in the late 1980s.

WILLIAM ARNE
Post-war German owner and rider.

SPEEDY BABBS
The first world endurance record holder for the Wall in 1929 and also a Globe rider.

JOE BARKER
Post-war rider riding with Messhams.

PIERRE MARIE BAUDRAS
French rider.

SPEEDY BAUER
Rode at Olympia in 1929.

NORBY BATCHELOR
Australian rider who rode from 1928 to 1957 around the Sydney area as one of the 'Speed Demons', presented by the Barcola Brothers.

JASON BATEMAN
Rode with the Messhams and the Motordrome Company.

DEREK 'BLASTER' BATES
Wall rider, Second World War bomber pilot and demolition expert.

WILLIAM BELLHOUSE – 'CYCLONE BILLY'
Sheffield speedway rider who went on to become both a Wall and Globe rider, ending his career in 1935 after a serious accident.

GUIDO BERGO
Italian rider, rode with Messhams, 1972.

RIDING THE WALL OF DEATH

MARK BLACKWALL
Rode with Tommy Messham.

TIM BLACKWALL
Also rode with Tommy Messham and died in car crash. Brother to the above.

MARTIN BLOOMER
German rider who held the record for riding the Wall in the *Guinness Book of Records*.

KEITH BONNER
Rode for the Todds in the 1950s.

VICKY BONNETT
Ex-nanny who rode for the Cripseys in the 1990s.

BILLY BUTLIN
Entertainment entrepreneur responsible, along with Pat Collins, for picking up on the Wall and establishing its popularity in the UK.

NEIL CALLADINE
Fairground archivist and spieler for The Ken Fox Troupe.

KERRI CAMERON
Woman rider with the Ken Fox Troupe.

BOB CAREW
Early American rider, one of the first to ride a Wall in Europe.

PETER CATCHPOLE
Owner and rider of many Walls.

SERGEI CHITYAN
Russian rider who rode for Tommy Messham and later had his own Walls in Aberavon and Porthcawl.

CRAZY CLAIRE
Rider with the Ken Fox Troupe

NOBBY CLARKE
Rode for Jake Messham in the 1950s.

PAT COLLINS
Fairground maestro responsible for encouraging the Wall in the early years and establishing it as a mainstream attraction.

'WALSALL' JOHN COLLINS
Adopted son of Pat Collins and his ultimate heir. Owned and ran Walls and Globes.

RECKLESS RUDY COOMBS
Described as 'The World's Most Daring Trick and Fancy Rider' in the late 1920s.

HENRI CORBIERE
Early French Globe of Death rider.

GRAHAM CRIPSEY
Roy Cripsey's son, Wall rider who went on to become a professional snooker player before reviving a Wall in the 1990s.

ROY CRIPSEY
Early Wall rider who travelled a Wall before running a static Wall in Skegness.

ROY CRIPSEY JNR.
Straight and trick rider and Wall owner. One-time owner of the Messham Wall.

HUGO DABBERT
Holder of the world endurance record of over six hours, set in 1980.

DANNY DARE
Rider with the Ken Fox Troupe, distinguished by his many tattoos, including one of a Wall of Death. Rode with a Wall owned by J. Stan that travelled Thailand 1999-2005.

DIXIE DARE
1950s Wall rider.

KETRING DARE
American rider with a claim to be the first to drive a car on the Wall.

WALL OF FAME

PATSIE DARE
Pioneer skater and car rider at Olympia 1930/31.

GERRY DE ROY
Real name Gerry Jones, in the *Guinness Book of Records* as the oldest Wall of Death rider.

KEN DE WOLF
Rider with the Motordrome Company in the 1980s and 1990s.

FEARLESS EGBERT
Early American rider riding in Europe and one of the first to use lions.

BETTY ELLIS
Post-war woman rider who rode with and for most of the main Wall operators with her husband Cliff up until their retirement in the 1970s.

CLIFF ELLIS
Rode with wife Betty Ellis with most of the main Wall operators.

ALBERT EVANS SNR
Globe and Wall rider and owner in at the beginning of the Wall.

ALBERT EVANS JNR
Son of the above, trick rider and Wall owner still operating as a travelling showman.

EMILY EVANS
Albert Evans snr's wife, also rode the Wall.

HUMBERTO FONESCA
Brazilian Globe rider touring the US in the early 1980s.

AARON FORD
Tank rider.

ALLAN FORD
Trained with Tommy Messham and went on to ride with Yvonne Stagg and to revive the Wall of Death in the late 1980s with his Motordrome Company. Also a Globe rider.

KEN FOX
Wall owner and builder, operator of the Ken Fox Troupe, still travelling extensively in the UK.

LUKE FOX
Son of the above, current Wall rider.

BILLY FREEMAN
Welsh rider who became a regular at the Barry Island Wall in the 1950s.

JULIE FRENCH
Rode with Tornado Smith at the Kursaal after the Second World War and performed the 'Gymkhana Girl' stunt.

LAURIE GIMBRETT
Rode at the Kursaal, Southend with Yvonne Stagg 1964-1973. Last person to be taught be Tornado Smith. Now runs a driving school in Southend.

ANTHONIUS FREDERIKUS GOEMAN
Ex-president of the European Showman's Guild. Dutch Wall and Globe rider in the post-war period.

CHRIS GOOSEN
Irish Wall owner in the 1950s.

DORIS GRAY
Early 'Loop of Death' rider.

ADRIAN HASTINGS
Globe rider/owner, 1980s to present.

ELIAS HARRIS
Son-in-law to Pat Collins and a rider on Pat's Wall in 1930. Later presented Walls in his own right.

ROBBY HAYHURST
Early rider who joined Bob Carew and Kitty O'Neill who toured Europe and Russia in the 1930s.

RIDING THE WALL OF DEATH

HARRY HOLLAND
One half of a post-war Wall double act with Roy Swift at Belle Vue in Manchester, who went on to tour Europe and retire to New Zealand.

JEAN HOLLAND
Wife of the above, also rode just after the Second World War.

KEN HOOD
Wall owner, rider and operator. Later went on to run a flea circus.

GUNBOAT JACKSON
Black American rider who operated a one-man show at the Southend Kursaal in the early days.

RED JUETT
Rode a Silodrome Wall at the Kursaal, Southend 1929-1935.

NED KELLY
Stalwart of the Motordrome Company in the 1980s and 1990s, also rode with the Ken Fox Troupe and in Germany.

GUSTAV KOKOS
Austrian Wall owner and rider. Rode with Yvonne Stagg at the Kursaal, Southend and Dreamland, Margate. Murdered by Stagg's lover.

MEINDERT KREKEL
Dutch rider whose father owned a Wall. Rode from 1960 when aged twelve.

HENNY KROEZE
Speedway and Wall rider.

DUTCH JOHNNY
Rode briefly for Tommy Messham before riding in Holland. Died of a heart attack during a show.

RUDY KNIGHT
Rode in the 1920s and '30s with Miss Johnson.

JIMMY KYNASTON
Perhaps one of the best Wall riders ever, died in Sierra Leone.

JACK LANCASTER
Wall rider, married Gladys Souter.

BILLY LEE
1930s rider.

BOB AND MILDRED LEE
Husband and wife riders on Pat Collins' Wall from 1935.

CHRIS LEE
Trained by Tommy Messham, one of the best trick riders still operating today.

FREDDIE LEE
Rode for Tommy Messham in the 1970s.

PITT LOFFELHARDT
Legendary pre and post-war German Wall owner and rider, originally a racing driver.

JACK McMINN
Irish Globe owner and rider in the 1940s and '50s. Sold his Globe to Messham snr.

SPEEDY McNISH
American rider and Wall owner, rode with Speedy Babbs.

DOUGLAS MAC VALLEY
Globe rider riding in the early 1980s in Las Vegas. Currently living in New Zealand, he now owns many of the Globes in America.

FRANCIS MANDER
Wall rider and owner in the 1950s.

HEINZ MEINERS
German rider who rode from before the Second World War for over fifty years.

ARNO MIERS
Armless Wall rider from Litchfeld.

WALL OF FAME

JAKE MESSHAM
Owner, rider and operator pre and post-war.

JAKE MESSHAM JNR.
Current Wall rider with father James.

JAMES MESSHAM
Current Wall owner and rider.

NATHAN MESSHAM
Current Wall rider with father James.

JOY MESSHAM (NÉE LEGGIT)
Tommy Messham's wife, also a rider.

TOMMY MESSHAM
Son of Jake Messham, Wall legend responsible for training many post-war riders. At one point owned the only travelling Walls of Death in the UK.

TOMMY MESSHAM JNR
Third-generation Wall rider. Briefly revived an interest in the Wall in the 1990s.

BILL MILLER
One of the owners of the New Brighton Wall, also a rider.

JULIET MITCHELL
Rode with Tornado Smith in 1954 when only seventeen.

EDDIE MONTE
Wall rider and owner, sold Wall to Tommy Messham snr.

SAMANTHA MORGAN
American rider.

RONNIE MOORE
Famous New Zealand speedway rider who went on to become a Wall rider.

KITTY MULLER
German female rider pre and post-war, rode with Pitt Loffelhardt.

DOUG 'MILEAWAY' MURPHY
Post-war Lancashire rider who travelled Europe, the USA, Israel and Russia, with a particularly strong reputation at the Oktoberfest in Germany.

JIM MURPHY
Rode at the Kursaal, Southend 1964-1970.

SAM NAISHTAD
Manager and promoter of the Wall during its glory days and mentor to many early riders.

NIALL O'CONNOR
Globe rider and owner, 1980s to present

KITTY O'NEILL
Early female rider, toured Europe and Russia with Bob Carew and Robby Hayhurst in the 1930s.

CHRIS O'SULLIVAN
Tommy Messham rider, died in suspicious circumstances at Norwich Christmas Fair.

DOUG OLIVER
Rider in UK and Germany, went with Peter Catchpole's Wall to Sierra Leone. Known as Doug 'Speedman' Oliver.

CHRIS PALMER
Bought Cripsey's Wall of Fear in 2005 and restored it to allow it to be presented at selected events in Britain.

JOE PALMER
Son of Chris Palmer and current Wall rider.

RICHARD PALMER
Nephew of Chris Palmer and current Wall rider.

HORACE PARKER
Rode with brother Len as part of Marshall's Modern Amusements, went on to ride for Roy Cripsey.

SONNY PELAQUIN
Post-war American Wall owner and rider.

RIDING THE WALL OF DEATH

JACK PERRY
One of the American Perry family of Wall owners that also included Bob and Marion, famous for featuring their lion King on the Wall.

SPEEDY PHILL
Rode with Charles Winter.

JACK PINE
Rider in the 1940s, also rode with Tom Davis Trio.

EARL PURTLE
Early American Wall rider, originally a dirt-track rider, and one of the pioneers who brought the Wall to Europe.

PETER RAFFERTY
1950s Wall rider.

GINGER JOE REGAN
Rode with Francis Mander, now married to Betty Ellis

RESTALL BROTHERS
Canadian Wall riders, responsible for introducing the Souter sisters to the Wall of Death.

ROB RICHARDSON
Rode with the Motordrome Company.

JIM RICHES
Rode at Skegness and worked on Wild Mouse ride.

RHETT ROTTEN
Contemporary American Wall rider.

HAZEL RUSSELL
Rode with Speedy Bauer at Olympia in 1929.

ALBERT SEDGEWICK
Rider with Albert Evans.

ALMA SKINNER
One of the first women Wall riders, started with Billy Butlin, known as 'Dare Devil Alma'.

HECTOR 'SKID' SKINNER
Husband to the above, ex-speedway rider who went on to operate the Bombshells troupe and to gain superstar status.

GARY SYKES
Rider with the Motordrome Company in the 1990s.

EDDIE SLOANE
Globe rider and owner, 1980s to present.

TORNADO SMITH
One of the greatest Wall showmen, known in particular for his publicity stunts and use of a lion, operated out of the Kursaal in Southend until the 1960s.

SOOTY
Real name Wayne Pert, black rider with Messhams. Rode in Holland with Bloomers. An excellent Wall cyclist.

GLADYS SOUTER
Originally one of three women (including Winnie Souter) known as the 'Wizards of the Wall' operating in Scarborough. Later toured Germany. Married Jack Lancaster.

JACK SOUTER
Brother to Gladys and Winnie. Rode with Winnie and George Todd when they needed a third rider after buying their own Wall. Rode at Dreamland after the Second World War.

WINNIE SOUTER
Also one of the original 'Wizards of the Wall'. Later toured Scotland where she met and married George Todd. Together they bought their own Wall in 1936.

WALL OF FAME

GODFREY SPARGO
Great supporter of the Wall of Death over the years and driving force behind the Boxford Revival in 1999. Went on to manage speedway teams.

YVONNE STAGG
Took over Tornado Smith's Wall at the Kursaal and rode with her partner Gustav Kokos. Committed suicide.

LAURIE STAIG
Wall and Globe rider, also a clown.

ANNABELLE SWIFT
Driver with Ken Fox Troupe.

MAUREEN SWIFT
Post-war female rider who started aged fifteen and had her own Wall aged eighteen. Went on to ride in Germany.

ROY SWIFT
Rode as part of a double act with Harry Holland at Belle Vue in Manchester.

HELMUT SZMIDT
Known affectionately as 'Helmet', a German rider from the 1950s to the 1970s who died building up a rollercoaster when someone sent a car down it.

LUCKY THIBEAULT
American Wall, Globe and Cage of Death rider who started with his own Wall in 1949 and began riding again in the late 1980s after a twenty-five-year gap.

LOWELL THOMAS
American Rider from the mid-1930s to 1965 who did the riding for the Elvis film *Roustabout* on his own Wall.

BOB TODD
One of the four Todd brothers on the Wall in the 1930s – used to be towed round on roller skates.

FRANK TODD
Owned own Wall before the Second World War that he lost in Italy when on tour. Also had a Wall in England after the war.

GEORGE TODD
One of the four Todd brothers who owned a Wall before the Second World War. Rode at Dreamland after the war.

JACK TODD
One of the three Todd brothers who owned a Wall before the Second World War and one of Pat Collins' riders in 1929, becoming his principal rider the following year.

THE VARANNE BROTHERS
Danny, Philippe and Gerard, presenters of a Globe and Wall act in France.

VIVIENNE TODD
Female Wall rider married to Frank Todd.

BILLY AND MARJORIE WARD
Pioneer husband-and-wife team who toured South Africa and came to the UK in 1929, later performing at the Belle Vue in Manchester.

ALBERT 'CYCLONE' WATSON
Pre-war rider based in Nelson, Lancashire.

GARRY WHITEHEAD
Irish Globe rider in the 1940s and '50s

JIM 'WHIRLWIND' WHITTINGHAM
Rider in the 1930s.

BILLY WILLIAMS
Irish-Canadian rider who rode Pat Collins' Wall at Dudley Carnival Fair in September 1929.

MAY WILLIAMS
Wife of the above, part of a double act with her husband.

CINDY WILLIS
Rode at the Kursaal, Southend 1960-1970.

RIDING THE WALL OF DEATH

CHARLES WINTER
Globe and Wall rider, still riding today.
Expert bike restorer specialising in Indians.

HERBERT WISSINGER
German owner and rider.

TONY WRIGHTON
Wall rider in the 1950s.

KAPTAIN WULFHURST
Wall rider in Germany, 1930s.

Others worthy of mention include the following, many of whom are known more by reputation than name:

BETTY ALLEN

PETER BARROW

ANDY BURLEY

MIKE DE BIDUPH

KIP GREEN

KEVIN HAINES

VINCE LEE

MICK'S MOTORCYCLES

JIMMY PARKER

IAN TIDY

RICHARD WILSON

SOURCES

Writing this book has meant consulting a wide range of sources in addition to the extensive Wall of Death archive held by Allan Ford. The authors would particularly wish to thank those individuals who gave so freely of their time and memories to help us put the Wall's story together, including:

> Keith Bonner, rider in the 1950s
> Neil Calladine, Wall of Death historian
> Gerry Jones (Gerry de Roy), post-war Wall rider
> Betty Ellis, post-war Wall rider
> Ken Fox, rider from the 1970s to the present day
> Neil Smart (Ned Kelly), rider in the 1980s and 1990s
> Chris Lee, rider from the 1970s to the present day
> James Messham, Tommy Messham's nephew and current Wall owner
> Chris Palmer, Wall owner in 2005
> Roy Swift, rider in the 1950s
> Charles Winter, rider of Walls and Globes from the 1980s
> Ann Wright, daughter of Winnie Souter and George Todd

We would also like to thank Vanessa Toulmin and Ian Trowell of The National Fairground Archive for their assistance.

In addition, we have consulted a number of published sources and websites and the following lists highlight the main sources used:

BOOKS:

Freda Allen and New Williams, *Pat Collins: King of Showmen*, (Uralia Press 1991).
Frances Brown, *Fairground Folk: A History of the British Fairground and its People*, (Malvern Publishing Company 1986).
John Carroll, *The Legend of Indian*, (Grange Books 2001).
William L. Gresham, *Monster Midway*, (Victor Gollancz 1954).

Peter Haining, *Tornado Smith: Wall of Death Pioneer*, (Boxford Community Council 1998).
Barry Norman, *Human Flies Cheating Gravity and Death*, (WKVL Amusement Library 1995).
Joe Scalzo, *Evel Knievel and Other Daredevils*, (Tempo Books 1974) – chapter on Speedy Babbs.
Garry Stuart with John Carroll, *Indian*, (Osprey Automotive 1994).
Roland Opschondek, Florian Dering, Justina Schrieber, *Im Banne Der Mototen*, (Buchendorfer Verlag 1995).
Michael Ware, *Historic Fairground Scenes*, (Moorland Publishing 1977).
Ned Williams, *Fairs and Circuses in the Black Country*, (Uralia Press 1994).
Peter Wilkes, *The Great Nottingham Goose Fair*, (Trent Valley Publications 1989).

WEBSITES:

www.ammh.nl – Site for the American Motorcycle Museum based in Holland.
www.globeofdeath.biz/us/globe.html – Site for the Varanne brothers' Globe of Death.
www.globe-of-death.com – Site for Globe show based in Preston, Lancashire.
www.globeofdeath.com – American Globe with site featuring original patent for a Globe dated 1904.
www.indianmotorbikes.com – Features short biography of American rider Sonny Pelaquin.
www.indianriders.co.uk – Site dedicated to Indian Motorcycles.
www.originalwallofdeath.com – Site for Chris Palmer's Wall (New Wall).
www.thewallofdeath.com – Allan Ford's website.
www.wall-of-death.co.uk – Ken Fox's website.
www.wallofdeath.net – General Wall of Death site.
www.wallofdeath.com – Site for US Rider Rhett Rotten, including video of Rhett riding.

INDEX

NOTE: Riders not mentioned by name in the Index may feature in the Wall of Fame section

Abbins Brothers, Paulitt and Henri 29, 76, 79, 84, 149
American Amusement Company 26
Anderson, Sam 19
Armstrong, Erle 17
Austin Cars 62, 63, 69, 96
Auto Rides Ltd 27
Babbs, 'Speedy' 25, 80, 83, 130, 149, 152
BMW motorcycles 60, 61, 123
BSA motorcycles 60, 61, 115, 119, 120, 124
Barry Island 44, 107, 151
Bauer, 'Speedy' 38, 149, 153
Battersea 90, 91, 120, 131
Belle Vue, Manchester 28, 50, 63, 93, 95, 98, 151, 154, 155
Bellhouse, William 'Cyclone Billy' 26, 30, 38, 77, 82, 149
Bertram Mills Circus, Olympia 44, 82, 98
Bicyclist's Globe, US Patent 77, 78
Bombshells 38, 154
Bonnett, Vicky 124, 138, 150
Botha, George 22
Boxford 42, 43, 46, 139, 140, 154
Bowl of Death 14, 75, 82, 86
Butlin, Billy 26, 32, 34, 36, 38, 40, 50, 82, 96, 103, 105, 138, 150, 154
Buxford Steam Group 138, 142
British Empire Exhibition 24, 75, 148
Campbell, Malcolm 24, 25, 27, 126
Cars on the Wall 26, 36, 49, 50, 62-6, 95
Carew, Bob 32, 53, 150, 151, 153
Catchpole, Peter 68, 93, 100, 103, 105, 108, 116-120, 122-4, 129, 138-9, 142, 150, 153
Chityan, Sergei 122-3, 150
Cody, 'Cyclone Jack' 27, 30,
Cody, 'Suicide Lou' or Curly 38, 39, 48
Collins, 'Walsall John' 76, 79, 84, 150
Collins, Pat 32-33, 40, 63, 77, 81, 82, 90, 107, 112, 150, 151, 152, 154, 155, 157
Corbiere, Henri and Elizabeth 79, 80, 150
Crawford, Pauline and Red 27, 30
Cripsey, Frankie 124
Cripsey, Gary 122
Cripsey, Graham 124, 138, 150
Cripsey, Roy 96, 98, 105, 106-8, 122, 124, 126, 141-2, 150, 153

De Roy, Gerry 8, 105-8, 129, 131, 140, 151, 158
Death Ring, British Empire Exhibition 24, 75, 76
Deaths on the Wall 72-73
Desnos, Bill 27
Dips and Dives of Death 12, 69, 95
Eat the Peach 143-4
Egbert, Fearless 32-3, 151
Ellis, Betty 98-9, 105, 151, 153, 157
Ellis, Cliff 100, 151
Evans, Albert, jnr 8, 27, 97, 105, 106, 111, 151
Evans, Albert, snr 27, 29, 35, 41, 73, 75, 76, 96, 97, 100, 103-7, 110, 122, 137, 140, 151
Festival of Britain 91, 96, 120
Ford, Allan aka 'Fearless' 22, 61, 68, 70, 72, 84, 85, 105, 107, 108, 115, 122, 125, 128, 131, 139, 140, 142, 147, 149, 151
Fox, Ken 61, 71, 79, 95, 106, 108, 116, 124, 129-131, 139, 142, 147, 151, 157
French, Julie 101, 151
Globe of Death 8, 29-30, 33, Ch. 5, 94, 95, 100-1, 139, 143, 149-151, 154
Go-karts on the Wall 65
Goddard, Charles 19
Gorky Park 125, 137
Grave, Tom 15
Grant, Billy 35, 50, 51
Green, John 40
Hall and Wilson Trio 19, 20, 75
Hamburg Domfest 49, 80, 92, 125
Harley Davidson motorcycles 61
Harris, Elias 33, 90, 106, 112, 151
Hastings, Adrian 88
Hayhurst, Robby 53, 151, 153
Hell Drivers Race 24, 91
Heywood, Freddy 97
Holidays at Home 90
Holland, Harry 93, 95, 107, 120, 151, 154
Honda motorcycles 61, 62, 71, 73, 86
Indian Motorcycle Company 58, 59, 61, 69, 77, 84, 92, 95, 107, 115, 120, 137
James, motorcycles 59, 84, 87
Jones, Charles Henry 12-15
Jones, Gerry 105, 151, 157, see Gerry De Roy

RIDING THE WALL OF DEATH

Jones-Hilliard Bicycle Sensation 13, 19
Kelly, Ned *see* Neil Smart
Kelvin Hall, Glasgow 27
Ketring, Earl 42, 92
Ketring and Dare 52, 54, 64
Kokos, Gustav 60, 100, 108, 119-120, 152, 154
Kursaal, Southend 27, 43, 44, 46, 50, 92, 98, 100, 108, 120, 151, 152, 154
Kynaston, Jimmy 118, 119, 123, 152
Lambretta, scooters 61
Lee, Chris 70, 72, 73, 105, 129, 131, 140, 142, 147, 152, 157
Lee, Freddie 72, 105, 152
Lee, 'Speedy Bob' 38, 48
Levis, motorcycles 20-22
Lions, use of on Wall 26, 32, 42, 50, 53, 101, 151
Liondrome 50, 101
Locock, Tom 15
Löffelhardt, Pitt 48, 49, 101, 152, 153
Loop of Death 100, 151
Lowcock and Grave 15
MacValley, Douglas 86, 152
Manders, Francis 107, 120
Marchington, Tony 129
Margate 119-121, 125, 152
Mathieu, Kitty 120
Meiners, Heinz 48, 49, 101, 152
Merrie England, Ramsgate 27, 50, 66, 90, 99
Messham, Jake 35, 93, 94, 96, 97, 100, 112, 116, 118, 122, 152
Messham, James 142
Messham, Joy 106
Messham, Tommy, jnr 72, 124, 138
Messham, Tommy snr 73, 79, 81, 84, 86, 89, 91, 96, 103, 105-8, 111-7, 122, 130, 139, 140, 142, 144, 147, 152
Miers, Alf 50, 51, 152
Monkeydrome 54
Monte, Eddie 35, 40, 91, 100, 105, 112, 142, 153
Moore, Ronnie 98, 153
Motoguzzi, motorcycles 115
Motordrome Company, The 126, 128, 129-31, 142, 149, 151, 152, 153, 154
Motordromes 17, 19, 25
Muller, Kitty 48, 49, 99, 101, 153
Munich 40, 48, 60, 62, 92, 100, 117, 125, 136
Murphy, Doug 22, 65, 92, 105, 106, 108, 116, 118, 122, 148
Naishtad, Sam 19, 40, 79, 153
New Brighton 31, 32, 38, 50, 95, 97, 98, 100, 118, 153
Olympia 42, 44, 50, 52, 54, 64, 80, 82, 98, 149, 151, 153
Orton and Spooner 35, 36, 40, 42
O'Connor, Niall 86
O'Neill, Kitty 53, 151, 153
O'Sullivan, Chris 106, 153
Oktoberfest *see* Munich
Oliver, Doug 118, 153
Palmer, Chris 141, 142, 153, 157
Parker Amusement Company 19
Parker, Horace 153

Len Parker 72, 97
Pelaquin, US Wall family 101, 153, 158
Perry, 'Captain Bob' and Marion 27, 28
Presley, Elvis 143
Purtle, Earl 25, 153
Race of Death 50, 52, 59, 70, 95, 105
Restalls, Canadian brothers 31-2, 153
Rolfe, Ron 82
Rollerskates, use of on Wall 52, 65, 66, 154
Royal Enfield Motorcycles 59, 100
Scarborough 32, 40, 63, 105, 164
Sedgwick, Albert 35
Showman's Guild 33, 111-2, 114, 138
Sidecars on the Wall 32, 34, 35, 46, 47, 50, 61, 62, 65, 79, 80, 98, 142
Silodrome 18, 19, 25-7, 29, 30, 35, 36, 75, 76-7, 79
Silodrome Company 33, 34, 36, 40, 43, 77
Silverstone, Joe 27
Skinner, 'Dare Devil Alma' 32, 38, 63, 98, 124, 154
Skinner, 'Skid' 38, 82, 143, 154
Sloane, Eddie 86
Smart, Neil aka Ned Kelly 8, 71, 130, 131, 137, 147, 152, 157
Smith, 'Brisbane' 62
Smith, 'Dynamite' Doris 44, 103, 151
Smith, 'Tornado' or George 42-6, 48, 50, 53, 59, 61-3, 79, 100, 103, 108, 116, 119, 120, 129, 138, 139, 140, 142, 148, 151, 154
Souter, Gladys 38, 152, 154
Souter, Winnie, aka 'Fearless Winnie' 30, 38, 39, 42, 89, 98, 99, 154, 157
Southsea 106, 107, 117
Spanish City 43
Speedway 17, 26, 31, 37, 38, 62, 92, 98, 143, 149, 152, 153, 154
Stagg, Yvonne 100, 103, 104, 108, 116, 118, 119, 120, 121, 151, 152, 154
Steam Motorcycle, on the Wall 61
Stuttgart Volksfest 125
Swift, Maureen aka Maureen Kelly 98, 99, 117, 123, 154
Swift, Roy 93-6, 98, 151, 154, 157
Tayleur, 'Garlicky' Bill 41-2, 102, 148
Thibeault, 'Lucky' 86, 87, 148, 154
Todd, Bob 66, 154
Todd, Frank 38, 91-2, 96-7, 107, 120, 154
Todd, George 32, 38, 40, 52, 89, 154
Todd, Jack 38, 109, 154
Tom Davis Trio 19, 20, 21, 22, 24, 75, 76
Triumph motorcycles 59, 61
Varanne Brothers, Danny, Philippe and Gerard aka The Infernal Varanne 88, 122, 127, 154, 158
Ward, Billy and Marjorie 24, 30, 52, 155
Whirl of Death 18, 19
Wickbold, Arno 84-6, 98-9
Williams, Speedy 32
Winter, Charles 8, 84-6, 107, 142, 144, 153, 155, 157
Wissinger, Herbert and Irene 99, 101, 155
Wizards of the Wall 26, 30, 32, 39, 48, 154
Yamaha motorcycles 86

If you are interested in purchasing other books published by The History Press, or in case you have difficulty finding any of our books in your local bookshop, you can also place orders directly through our website

www.thehistorypress.co.uk